A to I

The Journey of AI from Arrival to Implementation

Benjamin Rowe

First published in the United Kingdom in 2026 by BDRowe Consulting Ltd. (First Edition)

ISBN: 978 1 0369 6274 6
Edited by Dawn Adams
For more information visit www.benjaminrowe.com

Dedicated first and foremost:
to my wife, Lindsay,
and my boys, Sebastian and Jenson

Further thanks:
The friends and colleagues that have encouraged me along the way, and the amazing peer reviewers that helped shape the book and make it better than I could have imagined: Ian Hanahoe and Matthew T. I. Hill

Many thanks also to my editor, Dawn Adams, whose meticulous eye and thoughtful feedback strengthened this book in countless ways.

And to all the people that have shaped my career…
good and bad.

Preface

A note from the author

I set out on a simple mission: To deepen my understanding of modern AI. My aim was to acquire the skills and knowledge to deploy this rapidly evolving technology further personally and professionally. I also wanted to explore how I could best help my clients understand, in a practical business sense, translating this tech into language that's easy to understand. At the time, I thought what better way to learn about AI than to ask AI itself... A simple task! Or so I imagined.

I started asking lots of questions, reading lots of articles, and undertook training courses. I found I had learnt so much that it made sense to collate it. So, I decided to write a book about the practical uses of AI in business. What I learnt along the way is that AI is an excellent tool, but we are only scratching the surface. Of course, there are concerns about its use and how far we allow AI into our lives and decision-making. But we are now exploring in ways we never believed possible only a few decades ago – especially now, as generative AI joins a longer history of AI technologies already embedded in our lives.

The following pages are a labour of love. A battle between man and machine to create a book all about AI. The methods and AI tools discussed in this book played a role in shaping it, reflecting the very themes it explores, enhancing creativity, streamlining workflows, and providing insights. But from concept to completion, the value of human expertise, rational thinking, and intelligence – to create meaningful work – is paramount to its success and delivery.

It's not been a simple journey, or a quick one, but hopefully you'll find this as engaging and rewarding to read as it was for me to create.

The future of AI is fascinating, and by its own admission requires human intervention (at least for now), and serious considerations on ethics. But we are only at the start – and while humanity holds a range of conflicting views shaped by culture, bias, and ambition – it is ultimately up to humankind to determine its future.

About the author

Benjamin Rowe, CITP MBCS, is an IT executive and business strategist with three decades of global experience in driving technology innovation and change. As the founder of BDRowe Consulting Ltd, Benjamin specialises in delivering bespoke IT strategies and solutions for organisations of all sizes, helping them navigate the complexities of digital transformation with precision and foresight.

Throughout his distinguished career, Benjamin has held leadership roles across industries, including manufacturing robotics, energy, retail, FMCG, transportation, and technology. His expertise spans IT strategy, leadership, infrastructure modernisation, and governance. Recognised for his ability to align technology initiatives with business goals, Benjamin combines a hands-on approach with strategic insight to deliver impactful, and sustainable results.

Benjamin's professional achievements span strategic consulting, professional speaking, and published journalism. He has spearheaded cloud-first strategies, led critical infrastructure upgrades, and developed multiyear IT strategy and tactical plans. A strong advocate for continuous improvement, Benjamin champions innovation and builds collaborative, high-performing teams to deliver meaningful and lasting change.

A member of the British Computer Society and a Chartered Information Technology Professional, Benjamin is committed to advancing the field of IT. He complements his extensive experience through continuous professional development, holding certifications in corporate strategy, negotiation, and leadership from prestigious institutions such as Harvard University, the University of Glasgow, and the University of London.

In *A to I – The Journey of AI from Arrival to Implementation*, Benjamin draws on his project delivery experience to provide readers with actionable insights and practical guidance for implementing AI effectively. His dedication to bridging the gap between cutting-edge technology and real-world applications ensures this book is both a comprehensive resource and an inspiring call to action.

Worksheets, Guides, and Toolkits

To complement the insights provided in this book, I've created 10 practical worksheets, guides, and toolkits, available to download at www.benjaminrowe.com, to help you turn knowledge into action. From assessing use cases to ensuring ethical implementation, these tools are designed to guide you at every step of your AI journey. Look for references to each worksheet throughout the chapters and download them for templates, examples, or as resources for hands-on support.

The AI Revolution in Business: Unlocking the Future

Introduction

For me, Artificial Intelligence has been a lifelong fascination. Like many people, I watched futuristic films as a kid and wondered what the future held for us all. Now it's no longer a distant promise; it is here, embedded in the fabric of daily life and reshaping home, work, and industries worldwide.

This book traces the evolution of AI, from its origins to its current applications and future potential. It explores how AI is shaping industries today, the opportunities it creates for businesses, and where it could take us next.

By delving into history, current case studies, and future trends, this book aims to equip business leaders, policymakers, and technologists with the insights and tools needed to understand and harness AI effectively.

This book is structured to provide both a foundational understanding and practical guidance for implementation. From the philosophical roots of AI to its modern-day applications in industries like healthcare, finance, retail, education, and beyond, each chapter reveals how AI has evolved and where it's headed. Whether you're looking to implement AI in your organisation, understand its ethical implications, or anticipate its impact on global challenges, this book is your comprehensive roadmap.

Who this book is for

It's for innovators, decision-makers, and learners eager to leverage AI as a tool for growth and transformation. By the end, I aim to give readers a clear understanding of the importance of AI's history, its capabilities and limitations, and empower them to navigate the complex and dynamic landscape of Artificial Intelligence with confidence.

Why this book?

In a world increasingly driven by data and automation, organisations of all sizes are under pressure to adapt, or risk being left behind. While AI offers immense opportunities, it also presents challenges – ethical and societal dilemmas, workforce transitions, and the complexities of implementation. This book was written specifically to provide clarity amid the hype, helping you make sense of AI, consider how to use it meaningfully in your own world, and make more informed decisions.

Contents

Chapter 1: The evolution of AI

As with all good stories, we start our journey at the very beginning. The long history of Artificial Intelligence is one of curiosity, ambition, and groundbreaking discovery. From ancient myths about intelligent beings to today's cutting-edge technologies, and the possibilities just beginning to emerge, AI's evolution reflects our quest to replicate intelligence and creativity. We're going to trace that journey, from the early mythological days to highlighting key philosophical concepts, historical innovations, and the pioneers who transformed AI into a scientific discipline.

The philosophical foundations of AI

The origins of AI date back to ancient history. Across civilisations, texts and artefacts describe artificial beings designed to perform human-like tasks, some created by gods, others by human ingenuity. Ancient Chinese and Indian writings contain references to mechanical beings capable of mimicking human actions, demonstrating that the idea of artificial intelligence is not a modern invention but one that has fascinated cultures around the world for millennia.

This historical curiosity was not just reflected in myths and legends but also in early philosophy. The idea of intelligence, what it means to think, reason, and act, was central to many philosophical discussions long before technology had the potential to make these concepts a reality. Philosophers like Aristotle laid the groundwork for logic and reasoning, developing the idea of syllogisms, basic principles that formed the foundation for modern computational logic, such as: If "All humans are mortal" and "Socrates is a human", then "Socrates is mortal". Later, during the Enlightenment (a period spanning the 17th and 18th centuries), figures like René Descartes and Gottfried Wilhelm Leibniz shifted these ideas from abstract thought into the realm of scientific investigation, refining the way we think about intelligence, reasoning, and automation. Their contributions helped move artificial intelligence from mythology to a structured method of logic, paving the way for future generations to pursue humanity's long-held ambition of building machines capable of replicating human thought. This ambition remains today but is edging ever closer to reality. We will explore these ideas in more detail throughout this chapter as we connect historical curiosity with modern advancements in AI.

Let's take a step back to Greek mythology, where the idea of *automata* was first introduced. The myth of Talos – a giant bronze automaton built to guard the island of Crete – is one of the earliest stories of artificial beings. Talos was depicted as a mechanical sentinel capable of independent action, a clear precursor to today's interest in robotics and artificial intelligence. But the idea of artificial beings was not unique to Greek mythology.

The Chinese and Indian texts I referred to earlier contain stories of mechanical beings that could mimic human actions. In China, *The Liezi*, a Daoist text from around the 4th century BC, tells the story of Yan Shi, an engineer who presented King Mu of Zhou with a lifelike mechanical man. This automaton could walk, move its limbs, and even sing. When it startled the king by appearing too realistic, he ordered it to be dismantled, revealing an intricate system of gears and joints made from wood and metal.

In Indian mythology, texts such as the *Yuktikalpataru*, attributed to King Bhoja, describe mechanical devices, including self-moving statues used in temples and palaces. The Mahabharata even references Yantras, mechanical warriors used in battle. This shows that, even so long ago, we had an early curiosity with automation and engineered intelligence, well before modern robotics could even be contemplated.

While these stories involve divine or mystical elements, they reflect a lasting fascination with creating artificial life. Throughout history, engineers and classical philosophers have pondered these ideas, shifting the thought from mythology to structured thinking. Aristotle developed his principles of logic and reasoning, forming the foundation for symbolic reasoning in AI. While Plato's allegory of the cave hints at the philosophical dilemmas surrounding perception and knowledge. If machines could simulate human understanding, would they truly "know" or merely mimic knowledge? Would they "know" they were machines? These questions continue to shape debates in AI ethics today.

As we fast-forward to the Age of Enlightenment, when science, reason, and intellectual exploration flourished, intellectual curiosity about the mechanics of thought began to blend with scientific exploration. This period marked a shift from hypothetical mythology to realistic investigation. Philosophers like René Descartes introduced groundbreaking ideas about the separation of mind and body, arguing that the mind, distinct from the physical world, could be understood as a distinct entity, akin to a machine. Descartes' famous dictum, "Cogito, ergo sum" ("I think, therefore I am"), encapsulated his belief that rational thought was the essence of human existence. Gottfried Wilhelm Leibniz, a contemporary of Descartes, then made significant contributions to mathematics and logic. Leibniz's invention of the binary system – the foundation of modern computing – was pivotal in transforming abstract philosophical concepts into practical tools. He envisioned a "universal calculus", a system capable of representing all human knowledge through a logical framework, which is a forerunner to the algorithms driving today's AI.

During the Enlightenment, this period also saw the construction of mechanical devices that mimicked human actions, bridging the gap between the philosopher's ideas and technological experimentation. In the 18th century,

Jacques de Vaucanson created lifelike automata, including a mechanical duck capable of flapping its wings, eating, and even simulating digestion. Not long after this, in the 19th Century, Charles Babbage invented his Analytical Engine. Though never fully built during his lifetime, this early computational device incorporated features of modern computers, such as loops and conditional branching. Babbage's collaborator, Ada Lovelace, recognised its potential to perform tasks beyond arithmetic, dubbing it the first "general-purpose computer". Lovelace's insights hinted at the possibilities of programming machines to simulate cognitive functions. These inventions were marvels of engineering, demonstrating the potential to encode complex behaviours into mechanical systems.

The intersection of logic and computation

The 19th and early 20th centuries saw a convergence of philosophy, mathematics, and engineering, setting the stage for modern AI. Advances in formal logic – led by figures like George Boole – provided the mathematical framework for computational reasoning. Boolean algebra, a system of logic based on binary values (true or false), became the foundation for digital circuits and programming languages. Alan Turing, one of the most influential thinkers in AI history, integrated these ideas into a cohesive framework. In his 1936 paper, "On Computable Numbers", Turing introduced the concept of a

universal machine capable of performing any computation that could be described algorithmically.
This "Turing Machine" was a theoretical construct, but it showed that programmable devices could exist. Turing's 1950 paper, "Computing Machinery and Intelligence", posed the now-famous question, "Can machines think?". He proposed the Turing Test as a practical method to evaluate a machine's ability to exhibit intelligent behaviour indistinguishable from that of a human. In this test, a human evaluator interacts with a machine and another human through a text-based conversation, without knowing which is which. If the evaluator or evaluators cannot reliably tell the difference between the machine and the human, the machine is said to have passed the Turing Test.
While flawed, this concept remains a fundamental part of AI philosophy, as it explores how machines might mimic human perception, thinking, and communication in a way that feels natural and convincing. It wasn't until 2014 that a chatbot named Eugene Goostman became the first to convincingly pass the Turing Test, highlighting both the challenge and enduring relevance of Turing's original idea.
John Searle's "Chinese Room" experiment challenges the idea that AI can think or understand like humans. Searle imagined himself locked in a room with a set of instructions (written in a language he does not understand, for example Chinese) and a system for manipulating symbols. When given a question in Chinese, he uses the instructions to produce a correct response in

Chinese, even though he has no understanding of the language itself. Searle argued that this is how AI works: It follows programmed rules to produce responses but doesn't actually understand what it's doing.
This raises some big ethical questions. If AI can mimic human thought, does that make it the same as a human? Should it have rights? Should it be held responsible for its decisions? These were once abstract ideas – but today they matter more than ever – as AI is being used in self-driving cars, healthcare, and even military technology. Assigning responsibility is a huge area for discussion. Even if an AI system can act intelligently and pass tests like the Turing Test, Searle argued that it still wouldn't truly understand what it was doing. It would simply follow patterns and instructions, much like the person in the Chinese Room. This difference between *acting* intelligent and *being* intelligent is one of the most significant debates in AI today. Will machines ever achieve real understanding, or will they always be clever imitators?
These philosophical ideas behind the origins of AI have now moved beyond theory to shape real-world advancements in science and technology. Principles like logic, reasoning, and automation are built into the algorithms and systems. As AI continues to develop, these philosophical foundations help us understand its impact, create ethical guidelines, and inspire innovative solutions. This long journey of AI we've been through reflects our enduring curiosity about replicating intelligence. And

today, this ambition drives our technological breakthroughs – that were once the wild ideas of our imagination – proving that philosophy and engineering are not separate endeavours but connected paths to understanding the nature of intelligence.

The Dartmouth Conference

I mentioned Turing earlier, and he's certainly a well-known figure in the field, but while his ideas inspired a generation of researchers, the field of AI truly coalesced in 1956 during the Dartmouth Conference – regarded as the birth of Artificial Intelligence as a formal discipline. Organised by John McCarthy, Marvin Minsky, Nathaniel Rochester, and Claude Shannon, this historic meeting brought together a group of mathematicians, computer scientists, and cognitive theorists to explore the potential of creating machines capable of mimicking human thought processes.

The conference was the first time the term "Artificial Intelligence" was introduced. It was coined by McCarthy and established its foundational goals: enabling machines to reason, solve problems, and learn from experience. Attendees discussed and envisioned a future where computers could replicate human cognition, automate decision-making, and revolutionise a critical platform for defining the scope, challenges, and ambitions of AI as a scientific field. The Dartmouth Conference was spearheaded by some of the brightest minds of the era, whose combined expertise and creativity laid the intellectual foundation for AI.

These days, Turing is often referred to as the "grandfather" of AI, and John McCarthy its "father". McCarthy was instrumental in organising the conference and shaping its agenda, and he championed the idea that machines could simulate every aspect of learning and intelligence. McCarthy later developed the Lisp programming language and further cemented his legacy, as Lisp became a cornerstone for early AI research.

The other pioneers forged their own paths – equally as exciting and groundbreaking:

Marvin Minsky was a pioneer in AI and cognitive science. He contributed critical insights into how machines could emulate human reasoning. His work on neural networks and symbolic reasoning pushed the boundaries of what was technically feasible at the time.

Claude Shannon, renowned as the "father of information theory", brought a unique perspective to the conference. His work on binary logic and information processing provided the mathematical foundation for computer systems capable of handling complex tasks.

Nathaniel Rochester, a computer scientist at IBM, contributed his expertise in hardware and programming, helping bridge the gap between theoretical discussions and practical implementation.

These visionaries shared a belief that machines could one day replicate human intelligence. Their collaboration at Dartmouth created a shared vision that would guide AI research for decades to come – including identifying several key objectives that would define the trajectory of AI research. Although ambitious, these goals set the stage for groundbreaking advancements in fields as diverse as computer vision, language modelling, and autonomous systems.

This resulted in a clear set of priorities:

- ***Problem solving and reasoning***: Researchers wanted to build systems capable of solving mathematical problems, proving theorems, and making logical deductions, emulating the cognitive processes of human reasoning.
- ***Machine learning***: The ability of machines to learn from data and improve their performance over time was considered essential for developing intelligent systems.
- ***Natural language processing***: Enabling computers to understand and generate human language was a critical goal, as it would allow seamless communication between humans and machines.
- ***Robotics and perception***: The integration of AI into physical systems, like robots, required advancements in sensory perception, motor control, and environmental interaction.

In the years following the Dartmouth Conference, researchers made important strides in translating these concepts into practical applications. Early AI systems –

though limited by the computational power of the time – demonstrated the potential of machines to perform tasks previously thought to require human intelligence.

One of the earliest breakthroughs was "The Logic Theorist", created in 1956 by Allen Newell and Herbert Simon. This has been considered the first AI application, designed to prove mathematical theorems by imitating the way humans approach logic. The two men then developed the "General Problem Solver" in 1957, an ambitious attempt to create a program that could tackle a wide range of problems using heuristic search techniques. Even though it was considered well ahead of its time, its real-world applications were limited. But it did lay the foundation for future AI systems by demonstrating the potential of a general-purpose problem solver.

Meanwhile, language and interaction also advanced, with Joseph Weizenbaum introducing "ELIZA" between 1964 and 1966. Unlike those earlier programs, which focused on logic and problem-solving, ELIZA engaged users in conversation by simulating the responses of a psychotherapist. Although it relied on simple pattern matching rather than true understanding, its ability to create the illusion of meaningful dialogue was revolutionary and hinted at AI's future role in human-computer interaction. These early successes demonstrated that machines could emulate aspects of human cognition, sparking optimism and attracting greater funding to AI research.

The rise of symbolic AI

The late 1950s and 1960s saw a dominance of symbolic AI, also known as "good old-fashioned AI" (GOFAI). This focused on using explicitly defined symbols and rules to represent knowledge and solve problems. Symbolic AI was particularly effective in domains where rules and logic were well-defined, such as chess, mathematical reasoning, and expert systems. Early AI systems like Arthur Samuel's checkers program (1959) – and later chess-playing algorithms – demonstrated that machines could outperform humans in specific, constrained domains. And AI researchers developed programs that could emulate the decision-making processes of human experts in fields like medicine, engineering, and finance. Although symbolic AI laid the foundation for many AI applications, it faced limitations in handling ambiguous, dynamic, or unstructured environments. These challenges would later drive the development of alternative approaches, for example those we now know as machine learning and neural networks.

Despite the initial excitement and progress, AI research encountered significant obstacles by the 1970s. The field struggled with computational limitations. The hardware simply wasn't up to the job that we were trying to achieve. Expectations were high – but due to this and the lack of practical applications beyond narrow academic settings, many critics argued that AI had overpromised and underdelivered, leading to reduced funding and support. This period, known as the "AI Winter", forced researchers to reassess their approaches. The limitations of symbolic AI and rule-based systems became apparent, particularly in their inability to generalise knowledge or adapt to new scenarios. As a result, interest shifted toward more flexible, data-driven methods, setting the stage for the resurgence of AI in later decades.

While the Dartmouth Conference and its immediate aftermath did not produce all the envisioned breakthroughs, its legacy is undeniable. It established AI as a legitimate scientific discipline and provided a roadmap for future research. The interdisciplinary collaboration it fostered, blending philosophy, mathematics, computer science, and engineering, remains a hallmark of AI research to this day. And the conference's visionary goals – though ambitious – continue to inspire new generations of researchers and technologists. From Turing's philosophical inquiries to the practical milestones of the Dartmouth Conference, the birth of AI as a discipline marked the beginning of a journey whose limits we still don't fully understand – and one that may continue developing in ways we can't yet predict. Could AI be the last major invention humankind ever makes?

The early days: Symbolic AI and rule-based systems

We've now covered the first few significant milestones in symbolic AI, but let's delve a little deeper to truly understand why they were so groundbreaking. The Logic Theorist, created by Allen Newell, Herbert Simon, and Cliff Shaw in 1956, was referred to as the first AI program. It was designed to prove mathematical theorems by mimicking human problem-solving processes. This program achieved notable success by proving 38 of the 52 theorems in *Principia Mathematica*, a seminal work in mathematical logic by Alfred North Whitehead and Bertrand Russell. In some cases, the Logic Theorist even devised proofs that were more elegant than those originally presented by the authors.

The Logic Theorist demonstrated that machines could not only manipulate symbols but also apply logical rules to achieve intelligent outcomes. It also introduced concepts such as heuristic search, which has become fundamental to AI research. This success proved that human-like reasoning could be encoded into a machine, sparking optimism about the potential of symbolic AI. We briefly discussed the General Problem Solver (GPS) in 1957. Unlike its predecessor – which was tailored for mathematical theorems – GPS aimed to solve a wide range of problems by applying a general-purpose heuristic search. It broke problems into smaller subproblems, solved each one, and then combined the results to find a solution to the overall problem.

GPS was an ambitious attempt to create a truly versatile AI system. And while it achieved success in solving some structured issues, its capabilities were again limited. The program struggled with complex or ill-defined problems, highlighting the inherent challenges of symbolic reasoning. Despite these apparent limitations, GPS introduced essential techniques, like means-ends analysis, that influenced subsequent AI research.

The emergence of expert systems

During the 1970s, researchers shifted their focus from generalised problem-solving systems like GPS to specialised programs known as expert systems. These systems were designed to replicate the decision-making processes of human experts in specific fields. By coding domain-specific knowledge into a set of rules, expert systems could provide accurate and consistent advice or recommendations.

One of the most famous expert systems of this era was "MYCIN". Developed at Stanford University in the early 1970s – it was named in reference to the suffix applied to antibiotic medicines. MYCIN was designed to diagnose bacterial infections and recommend appropriate antibiotic treatments. The system operated by asking the user a series of diagnostic questions, applying its knowledge base of medical rules to infer likely diagnoses and suggest treatments. Remarkably, MYCIN regularly

outperformed human doctors in accuracy, demonstrating the practical utility of AI in specialised domains.
Another expert system, "DENDRAL", named after the term "Dendritic Algorithm", was also developed at Stanford. DENDRAL was used in chemistry to analyse mass spectrometry data and predict molecular structures. Its success in automating complex chemical analysis tasks showcased the potential for expert systems to revolutionise scientific research and industry.

The successes of programs like the Logic Theorist, GPS, and expert systems highlighted the strengths of symbolic AI in solving problems within well-defined criteria. These systems excelled at tasks that required clear, logical reasoning. By explicitly coding human knowledge into rules, symbolic AI provided a way to automate complex cognitive tasks.
However, symbolic AI had some significant limitations. It was built on strict rule-based systems, which made it inflexible when dealing with anything new or uncertain. If a problem fell outside its predefined knowledge, it simply could not adapt or make sense of it. Another challenge was the limited computing power of the 1950s and 1970s, which made it difficult to process complex rule sets or scale these systems effectively. Representing real-world knowledge was also tricky; turning human reasoning into symbols and rules proved to be an uphill battle. Intuition and common sense, which come naturally to people, cannot be easily translated into code. On top of that,

symbolic AI was static. It did not learn or improve from experience but relied entirely on pre-programmed knowledge, making it poorly suited for fast-changing, data-rich environments.

Symbolic AI may no longer be the dominant approach, but its influence remains strong in modern systems. Many AI models today combine symbolic reasoning with data-driven techniques, creating powerful hybrids that benefit from the strengths of both. Knowledge graphs, used by companies like Google and Amazon, help search engines and recommendation systems by mapping relationships between different pieces of information.

Explainable AI, or XAI, relies on symbolic methods to make machine learning decisions more transparent, helping people understand how and why an AI system reaches a particular conclusion. Rule-based systems are still widely used in industries like finance and healthcare, where they help with compliance monitoring and automated reporting. Beyond these applications, symbolic AI shaped the development of formal logic and heuristic search techniques, which continue to be essential in computer science and AI research.

Ambitious goals, groundbreaking achievements, and significant challenges marked the early days of symbolic AI and rule-based systems. The early programs demonstrated the potential of machines to emulate human reasoning, paving the way for future advancements. Although symbolic AI faced limitations

that eventually led to the rise of alternative approaches, its influence on the field remains profound.
By providing a framework for structured reasoning and problem-solving, symbolic AI established the principles that continue to guide AI research and development. Its legacy is a testament to the ingenuity of early researchers and a reminder of the importance of balancing ambition with practical limitations in the pursuit of artificial intelligence.

The machine learning era

So, now we find ourselves in the late 1980s and 90s. It's a time of Walkmans, dial-up internet – questionable fashion choices like shell suits, denim jackets and scrunchies – and of course, MTV. The Berlin Wall was falling, *The Fresh Prince* was rising, and *Star Trek: The Next Generation* was boldly going into a new kind of future on TV. Against that backdrop, the movies became obsessed with mimicking human intelligence. Films like *Blade Runner* (1982) and *War Games* (1983) explored whether artificial beings could have emotions or control over life and death situations, followed by *The Terminator* (1984) and *Total Recall* (1990), where AI gains self-awareness and virtual reality blends with human consciousness. And let's not forget the film that epitomises the idea of intelligent machines taking over the world and humans unknowingly living inside a simulation in the captivating *The Matrix* (1999).

Together, these themes kick-started the next wave of AI. This big shift away from traditional rule-based systems of the past led us to focus more on AI that could learn from data. As computing power improved and digital data became more accessible, machine learning emerged as a key focus in AI research. Unlike symbolic AI, which followed strict programmed rules, machine learning allowed machines to recognise patterns and make decisions based on experience rather than fixed instructions.

- ***Decision trees***: These algorithms use a flowchart-like structure to model decisions based on specific criteria, enabling machines to make predictions or classify data with remarkable clarity.
- ***Support vector machines (SVMs)***: Introduced in the 1990s, SVMs provided a robust method for classification and regression tasks. By mapping data to higher-dimensional spaces, they allowed for the separation of complex datasets.
- ***Clustering models:*** Algorithms such as the k-means clustering method enabled machines to group similar data points without requiring labels, paving the way for applications in market segmentation, image analysis, and more.

These methods empowered AI systems to handle a wider range of challenges, including those with less structured data or ambiguous rules. However, we still had a lot of ground to make up in the hardware scene. The computational power available at the time couldn't handle the level of workload we were trying to achieve.

The next stage was neural networks. They had been conceptualised as early as the 1950s, and they too experienced a resurgence during this era, thanks mainly to the work of researchers like Geoffrey Hinton. Neural networks – inspired by the structure of the human brain – were designed to process information in layers of interconnected nodes or "neurons". One of the most transformative breakthroughs came with the development of "backpropagation", a technique that allowed networks to adjust their weights based on errors in predictions. Hinton and his collaborators demonstrated that backpropagation could significantly improve the accuracy of neural networks, enabling them to tackle more complex tasks.

Despite these advancements, neural networks faced several limitations during this period. Once again, computational constraints still meant that training large networks was prohibitively slow, and the lack of sufficient data often hindered their performance. Nonetheless, these early neural networks laid the groundwork for the deep learning revolution that would follow in subsequent decades.

The adoption of machine learning in practical applications began to flourish during the 1990s. In finance, it helped detect fraud, assess risk, and even power algorithmic trading by analysing transaction patterns to spot unusual activity. In healthcare, early models supported doctors by analysing medical images and patient data, offering a glimpse into the future of AI-driven diagnostics. In manufacturing, predictive maintenance systems used machine learning to monitor equipment performance, helping reduce downtime and keep operations running smoothly.

While machine learning held great promise, the era faced significant challenges. Data collection and storage were expensive. In the 1990s, a few gigabytes could cost thousands, and hard drives were still measured in megabytes or even kilobytes. This made them insufficient for training large models, and yet again, that pesky hardware problem restricted the size and complexity of models that could be deployed effectively.

The scepticism surrounding AI during this period – stemming from the failures of symbolic AI – also limited investment and interest. These challenges delayed the widespread adoption of machine learning (ML), even as researchers laid the theoretical foundation for future breakthroughs.

The big data and deep learning revolution

The 2010s ushered in a paradigm shift in AI with the advent of deep learning – a subset of ML characterised by multilayered neural networks capable of processing vast amounts of data. This revolution was made possible by the convergence of four critical factors: the proliferation of big data, advancements in algorithms, the rise of GPU (graphics processing unit), computing, and the decreasing cost of storage and processing power, which made large-scale experimentation financially viable.

As the digital age progressed, the volume of data generated globally reached unprecedented levels. Social media, e-commerce, Internet of Things (IoT) devices, and online platforms produce massive datasets, providing the raw material needed to train deep learning models.

As the demand for more accurate and capable AI systems grew, large datasets became essential for training more advanced models. One of the most influential was ImageNet, a collection of millions of labelled images that set a new standard for computer vision research. Deep learning models trained on this dataset made huge leaps in image recognition – improving accuracy across various applications. Around this time, the rise of large text datasets also fuelled breakthroughs in natural language processing – enabling machine translation, sentiment analysis, and more sophisticated language models. These advances in these technology areas laid the foundation for deep learning's ability to move beyond basic pattern recognition, allowing it to process and understand complex data in ways that traditional methods could not.

Deep learning stood out from earlier AI methods because it could automatically recognise patterns in data. Convolutional neural networks (CNNs) became especially good at processing images, while recurrent neural networks (RNNs) helped with tasks involving sequences, like understanding text or predicting trends over time. A breakthrough came in 2017 with the introduction of the "Transformer" architecture, which changed the way AI processes language. Models like GPT and BERT – a model developed by Google to better understand the context and relationships between words in text– took advantage of this technology and made considerable improvements in answering questions, generating text, and understanding human language more naturally.

Training these deep learning models, however, requires a vast amount of computing power, which is why GPUs, originally designed for graphics, are ideal for training AI. The rise of GPU computing meant researchers could train larger and more complex models much faster than before. By the 2010s, deep learning was achieving things once thought impossible. And in 2011, IBM Watson beat human champions on Jeopardy!, proving that AI could process and understand natural language in real-time. In 2016, AlphaGo, developed by Google DeepMind, defeated world champions in the highly complex board game "Go", showing AI could master deep strategic thinking. Then came the rise of Tesla and other motoring companies, which began using deep learning in self-driving cars, bringing autonomous driving closer to reality.

Success in deep learning quickly spread across different industries. In healthcare, AI models like DeepMind's AlphaFold made groundbreaking discoveries in protein structures, helping speed up drug development. In retail, AI-powered recommendation systems transformed online shopping by personalising customer experiences. The media industry also changed, with AI generating everything from deepfake videos to automated news articles – reshaping how content is created and consumed. With these incredible new advancements, deep learning became a central part of everyday technologies, and ethical concerns began to take centre stage. These challenges span several critical areas, and this book delves deeper into these ethical dilemmas in Chapter 4, where we explore strategies for navigating the complex interplay between technology, society, and responsibility; however, here's a quick snapshot of some of those issues.

- ***Bias in AI models*****:** AI systems often inherit biases from the data they are trained on, leading to unfair or discriminatory outcomes. Biased facial recognition systems have shown lower accuracy for certain demographic groups, raising questions about fairness and accountability.
- ***Privacy issues*****:** The widespread adoption of AI in applications like social media, surveillance, and targeted advertising has heightened concerns about data privacy. AI-driven tools often collect and analyse vast amounts of personal information, prompting calls for stricter data protection regulations.
- ***Environmental impact*****:** Training large AI models requires significant computational resources, consuming enormous amounts of energy. This has sparked debates about AI's contribution to carbon

emissions and the need for more sustainable practices in the development of AI.

These ethical challenges are not merely academic; they have real-world implications that impact individuals, businesses, and society as a whole. Addressing these concerns has become a priority for researchers, policymakers, and organisations adopting AI.
With the groundwork laid by early philosophers, mathematicians, and computer scientists, AI was no longer just an idea; it was becoming a scientific discipline. But despite early breakthroughs, AI faced significant hurdles. The limitations of symbolic AI and rule-based systems led to setbacks, however, new approaches would soon emerge, bringing AI out of academic circles and into the real world. In the next chapter, we'll explore how AI transitioned from theory to practice and became an essential part of everyday life.

Chapter 2: AI today

As we reach the current stage of AI's evolution – the 2020s - AI is no longer a dream or a futuristic idea; it's an increasingly integral part of everyday life. It's in our phones, our homes, our workplaces, and the decisions being made around us. We ask voice assistants for the weather, streaming platforms suggest what to watch next, and businesses use AI to understand customers, spot trends, and even predict the future. After decades of research – trial and error, and a few false starts – AI has finally moved beyond theory into something practical and powerful. In this chapter, we'll explore how AI is shaping industries today, the key technologies driving it forward, and what that means for the world we live in.

Recent leaps in computing power, data availability, and algorithmic sophistication have advanced the rise of AI and its adoption. Today's AI systems are regularly referred to as "smart technologies" and excel in performing specific tasks with incredible precision and speed. Whether it's detecting fraudulent financial transactions, predicting consumer behaviour, or diagnosing diseases, AI is ingrained in many businesses. It allows us to make informed decisions and deliver tailored services to our customers. And the integration of AI into modern business processes has created opportunities that were unthinkable just a few decades ago. In industries ranging from healthcare and finance to retail, academia and manufacturing, AI is solving complex problems. However, the rapid adoption of AI has also raised big questions about its ethical implications, the impact on jobs, and the need for regulatory frameworks. As we continue to embrace AI, it's crucial to understand its capabilities and limitations, and to leverage its potential responsibly and effectively.

In its current state, the form most commonly known today is predominantly referred to as Narrow AI, also known as Weak AI. Unlike General AI – which aims to replicate human intelligence in its entirety – Narrow AI is designed to perform specific tasks by processing vast amounts of data, recognising patterns, and executing complex algorithms. It has become indispensable in modern business and technology, and the success of Narrow AI lies in its ability to process and learn from vast datasets. Machine learning, the backbone of Narrow AI, involves training algorithms on labelled data to identify patterns and make predictions. The more data these systems process, the better they become at their tasks, a phenomenon known as "scaling laws" in AI.

Take image recognition systems as a prime example; by analysing millions of labelled images, these systems learn to differentiate objects, identify faces, and even detect subtle anomalies. Similarly, recommendation engines improve their suggestions as they accumulate data on user behaviour, refining their predictions with every interaction. These algorithms behind Narrow AI are also highly specialised, designed to optimise performance for specific tasks. Decision trees, support vector machines, neural networks, and deep learning models are just a few of the techniques that enable AI systems to do exceptionally well in areas such as classification, regression, and clustering. These advancements have made Narrow AI remarkably versatile and effective, fuelling its rapid adoption across sectors.

The business impact of Narrow AI

One of the most significant advantages of Narrow AI is that it's good at doing what humans aren't good at, and what we usually don't enjoy – repetitive, time-consuming tasks that take a lot of effort and give little in return. It takes care of routine work like data entry, document review, and inventory management, freeing up employees to focus on bigger, more creative challenges. In customer service, chatbots and virtual assistants provide instant responses to queries, improving availability and helping businesses to engage with their customers 24/7. Streaming platforms, online retailers, and financial services all rely on AI-driven recommendations to personalise experiences, build loyalty, and drive revenue. Security and risk management have also seen a major shift thanks to Narrow AI. In finance and cybersecurity, AI models scan massive datasets in real time – spotting fraudulent transactions and suspicious activities faster than any human could. By continuously learning from new threats, these systems help businesses stay one step ahead of fraudsters and cybercriminals.

Despite its advantages, Narrow AI isn't without its limitations. Unlike human intelligence, it's designed to excel at specific tasks, but only those tasks. A fraud detection system – no matter how advanced – can't suddenly start diagnosing diseases unless it's completely retrained on new data. And that's another challenge: data dependency. AI models are only as good as the data they learn from. If the data is biased, incomplete, or misleading, the AI's predictions will be too. This can lead to real-world consequences – from unfair hiring decisions to flawed medical diagnoses – and it raises an important question we'll return to later: when things go wrong, who is really responsible?

Narrow AI also lacks context and common sense. It recognises patterns exceptionally well, but it doesn't truly "understand" them the way a human does. Ask it to handle a situation it wasn't specifically trained for, and it may struggle, produce unreliable results, or simply make it up.

While it has its limits, Narrow AI is far from reaching its peak. Advances in transfer learning, few-shot learning, and federated learning are pushing the boundaries – allowing AI to adapt to new tasks with far less training data than before. This means businesses will be able to deploy AI solutions faster and with greater flexibility.

Narrow AI may not be the holy grail of Artificial Intelligence, but it's the most practical, impactful, and widely used form of AI today. As businesses continue to integrate it into their operations, understanding its strengths, weaknesses, and future potential will be key to unlocking its full value. In practice, it's already part of everyday life. It's sorting your photos, writing your meeting summary, and is halfway through optimising your shopping basket, and you barely noticed!

Key technologies driving AI today

The rapid evolution of Artificial Intelligence is fuelled by a combination of innovative technologies that enable machines to understand, analyse, and generate complex data. These technologies are not only transforming how businesses operate but are also reshaping everyday experiences, scientific research, and creative endeavours. I've laid out some of the key technologies currently representing the pillars of AI's transformative potential to give an idea of what AI is currently capable of – and how far and wide it can be adopted.

Natural language processing (NLP)

As discussed earlier, natural language processing (NLP) bridges the gap between human language and machine understanding. It enables machines to process, interpret, and generate text or speech in a manner that feels natural to users. To give some context and examples:

- ***Sentiment analysis***: Businesses use NLP to analyse customer sentiment in reviews, social media posts, and feedback surveys. You've probably seen this most commonly on Amazon's product ratings. This helps gauge public opinion, summarise hundreds or thousands of reviews and improve customer experiences and satisfaction in purchases.

- ***Automated translation***: Tools like Google Translate leverage advanced NLP to provide real-time language translation. Modern translation systems use neural machine translation (NMT) models, which significantly improve the accuracy and fluency of translations.
- ***Document summarisation and classification***: NLP algorithms help summarise lengthy documents and classify text – streamlining processes in industries like legal, healthcare, and education.

Recent breakthroughs, such as the Transformer architecture, have revolutionised NLP – and common models like GPT (Generative Pre-trained Transformer) and BERT (Bidirectional Encoder Representations from Transformers) have been ingrained into everyday life. NLP can easily take tasks like text completion, question answering, and conversational AI and help us transform our thoughts, ideas and writing into a more comprehensible, structured, and engaging form. These advancements have enabled NLP to achieve near-human fluency in generating and understanding language. Despite these strides, challenges remain. Understanding nuances, idiomatic expressions, and cultural contexts are areas where NLP systems still struggle and need improvement. As researchers refine models and datasets,

NLP's capabilities will continue to expand – enabling more natural and effective human-machine communication.

Computer vision

Computer vision empowers machines to interpret and analyse visual data – enabling them to "see" and make sense of the world around them by using image recognition, object detection, and scene analysis. Here are a few areas where computer vision is in use and making inroads into helping us speed up or aid us in our day-to-day.

- ***Medical imaging*****:** AI systems equipped with computer vision analyse X-rays, MRIs, and CT scans to detect abnormalities such as tumours, fractures, or signs of disease. These tools enable radiologists to diagnose conditions with greater accuracy and speed.
- ***Autonomous vehicles*****:** Computer vision is a critical component of self-driving cars, enabling them to detect pedestrians, read traffic signs, and navigate roads safely. Tesla, Waymo, and other companies rely on advanced vision systems for real-time decision-making.
- ***Retail and manufacturing*****:** Retailers use computer vision for inventory management, theft prevention, and customer behaviour analysis. In manufacturing, AI-powered vision systems inspect products for defects, ensuring quality control.

- ***Consumer products***: Apple and Google are embedding computer vision into your phone's photo and video app so you can easily search for places, people, locations and even items in your albums.

Deep learning has significantly advanced the capabilities of computer vision, and Convolutional Neural Networks (CNNs) have revolutionised image recognition and object detection. Pre-trained models like ResNet, EfficientNet, and YOLO (You Only Look Once), deliver state-of-the-art performance in real-world applications.
Emerging techniques, like Generative Adversarial Networks (GANs), further enhance computer vision by enabling the generation and editing of images. These innovations are poised to push the boundaries of what computer vision can achieve – from realistic virtual environments to more precise medical diagnostics.

Reinforcement learning

Reinforcement learning (RL) is a type of machine learning where AI agents learn by interacting with their environment and receiving feedback in the form of rewards or penalties. Unlike supervised learning – which relies on labelled datasets – RL enables systems to discover optimal strategies through trial and error.

- ***Gaming***: RL has demonstrated remarkable success in mastering games that require strategic decision-making. OpenAI's Dota 2 bot and DeepMind's

AlphaGo have defeated human champions in complex games, showcasing the power of RL.

- ***Robotics*:** RL is widely used in robotics to train machines to perform tasks such as picking and placing objects, navigating environments, and assembling products. Boston Dynamics uses RL to enhance the agility and adaptability of its robots.
- ***Autonomous systems*:** From self-driving cars to drones, RL enables AI to make decisions in dynamic and uncertain environments. These systems learn to balance safety, efficiency, and performance while navigating complex scenarios.
- ***Personalised recommendations*:** Companies use RL to optimise recommendation engines, tailoring content and products to individual users based on their preferences and behaviours.

Recent advancements in RL have focused on scalability and efficiency with algorithms like Proximal Policy Optimisation (PPO) and Deep Q-Networks (DQN), which enable faster and more stable training of agents in complex environments. Transfer learning – where agents apply knowledge from one task to another – is also a promising area of research.

While RL has achieved notable successes, it remains computationally intensive and challenging to apply in real-world settings. Researchers are exploring hybrid approaches that combine RL with other techniques to improve scalability and reliability.

Generative AI

Generative AI is transforming the way we work, socialise and live our day-to-day lives by enabling machines to create high-quality content – including text, images, videos, and music. These systems leverage advanced neural networks to generate outputs that are becoming indistinguishable from human-produced work.

- ***Content creation***: Tools like GPT help create articles, reports, and creative writing pieces, streamlining workflows in journalism, marketing, and entertainment.
- ***Image generation***: Models like DALL-E create stunning visuals from textual descriptions – revolutionising graphic design, advertising, and product prototyping.
- ***Video and music production***: Generative AI is being used to compose music, create video content, and even produce deepfake videos for entertainment or malicious purposes.
- ***Healthcare***: In drug discovery, generative models simulate molecular structures, accelerating the development of new treatments.

The rise of GANs and Transformer-based models has fuelled the capabilities of generative AI. GANs consist of two networks – a generator and a discriminator – that compete to produce realistic outputs. In contrast, Transformer-based architectures like the latest GPT models, leverage massive datasets to generate coherent and contextually accurate text.

The technologies driving AI today – NLP, computer vision, reinforcement learning, and generative AI – are transforming industries and redefining what machines can achieve. Each represents a unique capability, from understanding language and interpreting visuals to learning strategies and creating content. Together, they form the backbone of modern AI. As these technologies evolve, they will continue to unlock new possibilities, but also new challenges. They transform businesses and society in profound ways, but also present new risks, responsibilities and ethical considerations, which we'll discuss later.

Applications across industries

Artificial Intelligence is emerging as a force across virtually every sector of the economy. By automating simple processes – allowing for better decision-making with easier-to-understand and quicker delivery of information – and delivering personalised experiences for the end customer, AI is creating unprecedented opportunities for businesses and individuals alike. I've captured a few specific examples to give a flavour of how AI is reshaping key industries. It's by no means exhaustive, but it is intended to provide an overview of the art of the 'possible' and how you could potentially utilise AI in your business.

Healthcare: Diagnosis, treatment, and patient care

In healthcare, AI is revealing new possibilities for enhancing patient outcomes, modernising operations, and advancing medical research. Its ability to analyse vast datasets and identify patterns makes it an invaluable tool for diagnostics, treatment planning, and personalised medicine.

- ***Diagnostics***: As we discussed earlier, AI systems can analyse medical imaging data such as X-rays, MRIs, and CT scans to detect conditions like cancer, fractures, and neurological disorders. Tools like Google's DeepMind have achieved diagnostic accuracy comparable to – and sometimes exceeding – that of expert doctors.
- ***Drug discovery***: AI can help to accelerate drug development by predicting molecular interactions and identifying potential candidates for new treatments. Insilico Medicine has used AI to design and validate drug molecules, significantly reducing research timelines.
- ***Predictive analytics***: By analysing electronic health records, AI can aid in predicting potential disease outbreaks, identifying at-risk patients, and informing preventive care measures. Hospitals are using predictive tools to allocate resources and plan interventions effectively.
- ***Virtual health assistants***: AI-powered chatbots and virtual assistants are supporting patients by

answering health-related queries, scheduling appointments, and reminding them to take medications. Several healthcare providers are offering virtual consultations powered by AI, which enables increased access to healthcare in underserved areas.

In the private sector, significant advancements have been made by some of the largest technology companies. Watson Health (formerly part of IBM, now operating as Merative under Francisco Partners) uses AI to assist oncologists by analysing vast medical literature and patient data. Its treatment recommendations are tailored to individual cases, ensuring evidence-based care. While there are still challenges in integrating these systems into everyday clinical workflows, Watson Health shows how AI can support and enhance human expertise in medicine.

The Mayo Clinic – renowned for its cutting-edge medical research and patient care – employs AI to bridge critical gaps in clinical trial participation. Clinical trials are essential for advancing treatments; however, matching eligible patients to the most suitable trials is a time-consuming and inefficient process. AI algorithms have transformed this challenge by automating and optimising the matching process. The AI systems analyse patient records, medical histories and diagnoses to identify individuals who meet the eligibility criteria for ongoing clinical trials. These algorithms can process vast amounts of unstructured data, such as doctors' notes and lab results, far more efficiently than traditional methods. The result is a significant increase in trial participation rates. Patients benefit from access to experimental treatments that may not be available otherwise, while researchers gain larger and more diverse participant pools, improving the validity of their findings. The Mayo Clinic has reduced the time it takes to validate new therapies, enabling the development and delivery of life-saving treatments to market more quickly. In fact, AI-assisted trial matching played a crucial role during the Covid-19 pandemic, when speed was essential in developing and testing vaccines and therapies.

Finance: Efficiency, security, and customer engagement

The financial sector was one of the first to embrace AI. They saw how easily and quickly data analysis could reduce risks and enhance customer experiences in their accounts and financial products. The ability to process and analyse – in real time – enables banks and financial institutions to make informed decisions and detect anomalies.

- ***Fraud detection***: The machine learning algorithms can analyse transaction patterns to identify fraudulent activities on customer accounts. These systems continually adapt, enhancing their ability to detect emerging fraud schemes. And PayPal's AI-powered tools process millions of transactions daily – to flag suspicious behaviour.

- ***Risk assessment*:** AI models can evaluate creditworthiness by using financial history, employment data, and spending habits. This means lenders can make faster and more accurate lending decisions while minimising their risk.
- ***Algorithmic trading*:** AI systems are being used to execute trades at optimal times by analysing market trends and historical data. High-frequency trading platforms rely on AI to maximise returns.
- ***Customer service*:** AI chatbots and virtual assistants are attempting to streamline customer interactions by handling simple enquiries related to account balances, transaction histories, and more. Erica – Bank of America's AI chatbot – successfully manages millions of customer queries, which has reduced the workload on the bank's customer service teams.

JPMorganChase is using AI to automate the review of legal documents, saving thousands of hours previously spent on manual analysis. Its COiN (Contract Intelligence) platform identifies key terms and clauses in contracts, which reduces errors and accelerates processes. Mastercard's AI platform is using machine learning to analyse patterns in transaction data. By comparing each transaction to millions of historical records, the system identifies anomalies that may indicate fraudulent behaviour. For example, if a cardholder's spending pattern suddenly deviates – such as a high-value purchase in a foreign country, or multiple purchases in different countries within a short period – it triggers a fraud alert. Fraudulent activities are a persistent challenge in the financial industry, with billions of dollars at stake each year. As the data is collected, these algorithms are continually improving, enabling the system to adapt to new fraud tactics. AI's speed and accuracy minimises false positives, making sure legitimate transactions are not unnecessarily declined while still flagging genuinely suspicious activity.

Retail and e-Commerce: Personalisation and optimisation

In the retail and e-commerce space, AI is playing a major role in changing the landscape by enhancing customer personalisation, streamlining supply chains, and optimising pricing strategies. Its ability to understand consumer behaviour and preferences has transformed how businesses interact with customers.

- ***Personalised recommendations***: The AI-driven recommendation engines analyse browsing history, purchase patterns, and demographic data to suggest products that align with their customer preferences. Amazon's recommendation system significantly contributes to its revenue by driving repeat purchases, which is based on customer browsing data.

- ***Dynamic pricing*:** Many retailers are using AI to adjust prices in real time based on demand, competition, and inventory levels. Airlines and event ticket companies are using this feature to attempt to optimise pricing strategies that maximise profits while maintaining customer satisfaction. There have been many criticisms of this pricing method in recent times, but the AI technology is performing as intended.
- ***Inventory management*:** Predictive analytics – powered by AI – is now helping retailers forecast their demand more accurately, reducing overstocking and stockouts. Walmart leverages AI to optimise its supply chain, ensuring products are always available at the right time of year and in the correct supply numbers.
- ***Augmented reality (AR) and virtual try-ons*:** AI-powered AR tools are a relatively new addition to the retail space. The technology has been around for a while, but it's only recently become affordable and widely adopted. This technology allows customers to visualise products before purchasing. Sephora's Virtual Artist enables users to "try on" makeup virtually, enhancing the online shopping experience.

In 2018, retailer Zara started integrating AI to analyse customer feedback and sales data, predicting trends and optimising inventory. This data-driven approach allows the company to respond quickly to market demands and maintain its competitive edge.

In the highly competitive retail sector, ensuring products are available when and where customers need them is critical. Walmart's AI systems analyse historical sales data – weather patterns, seasonal trends, and local events – to forecast demand for products across its vast network of stores. During hurricane season, the system may predict a spike in demand for bottled water, batteries, and emergency supplies in affected regions. This real-time analysis allows Walmart to adjust inventory levels proactively, ensuring shelves are stocked while minimising waste. Another area where AI plays a key role in Walmart's tech stack is its logistics operations. By optimising the delivery routes and warehouse operations, the company is reducing its transportation costs and shortening delivery times.

The use of all these AI systems and technologies translates into a more reliable shopping experience for customers. Products are more consistently available, and operational efficiencies contribute to better competitive pricing. These advantages help Walmart maintain its position as a leader in the retail industry while providing the service its customers expect.

Manufacturing: Automation, quality, and efficiency

AI is heavily integrated into modern manufacturing production lines – bringing improvements in productivity, quality control, and cost savings. By including AI in their robotics, predictive maintenance, and supply chain management, many manufacturers are revolutionising traditional processes.

- ***Predictive maintenance*:** Utilising AI systems to monitor machinery performance and predict potential failures ensures timely repairs take place and are scheduled effectively, which minimises unnecessary downtime. General Electric's Predix platform analyses sensor data from industrial equipment to optimise its maintenance schedules.
- ***Quality control*:** The computer vision systems powered by AI inspect products for defects, ensuring consistent quality standards in a fraction of the time. These systems are widely used in the automotive and electronics industries.
- ***Robotics*:** Collaborative robots, or "cobots", are working alongside human operators to automate repetitive or hazardous tasks. AI enables these robots to adapt to different environments and situations to improve efficiency – or carry out dangerous jobs
- ***Energy optimisation*:** AI-powered tools are analysing energy consumption in factories, identifying potential opportunities to reduce waste or using automated shutdown, which essentially lowers costs in both energy and maintenance. Siemens uses AI to optimise energy use across many of its manufacturing facilities.

Siemens has been at the forefront of integrating Artificial Intelligence into production processes. They are using AI-driven predictive maintenance systems to monitor machinery performance in real-time. Sensors embedded in factory equipment gather data on vibration, temperature, and pressure, which AI algorithms analyse to predict potential failures before they occur. This reduces downtime and extends the lifespan of critical assets. They are also employing AI to monitor and control energy consumption across their factories. These systems identify energy-intensive processes and recommend adjustments, helping Siemens to reduce its carbon footprint while cutting operational costs.
BMW has employed AI-powered vision systems to inspect car components during assembly, which ensures defects are detected early. This approach enhances product quality while reducing rework and waste – and essentially failures. The systems inspect products for defects with greater precision than human inspectors can, and AI can detect microscopic flaws in electronics or automotive components that were previously undetectable.

All the AI used in manufacturing enables a quicker and more reliable production line. This allows companies to produce their products more safely and cost-effectively, resulting in fewer defects. Consequently, customers receive a more reliable product, and manufacturers experience fewer returns due to warranty issues or defects.

Transportation: Navigating the future

AI is at the heart of the new wave of innovation in transportation, from autonomous vehicles to intelligent logistics systems. By enabling smarter navigation and resource allocation, AI is reshaping how people and goods are moved.

- ***Autonomous vehicles*:** Self-driving cars are using AI in their real-time decision-making, object detection, and route planning. Companies like Tesla, Volvo and Waymo are pioneers in developing AI systems that prioritise safety and efficiency.
- ***Ride-share platforms*:** Uber and Lyft rely on AI to optimise pricing, match drivers with passengers, and predict demand. These systems are enhancing the user experience while maximising profitability.
- ***Logistics optimisation*:** AI now analyses shipping routes, delivery schedules, and traffic patterns to improve efficiency in logistics. UPS's ORION system uses AI to reduce fuel consumption and delivery times.

DHL is leveraging AI-powered tools to monitor global supply chains, predicting disruptions and suggesting alternative routes. This approach means more timely deliveries and cost savings.
Tesla has revolutionised the transportation industry with its AI-powered Autopilot system, bringing the autonomous driving dream closer to reality. By combining

computer vision, neural networks, and real-time data processing, the autopilot function uses an array of sensors, cameras, and radar to gather data about the vehicle's surroundings. This data is processed by neural networks, which enables the system to recognise objects, detect lane markings, and attempt to predict the behaviour of other road users. The system provides features like adaptive cruise control, automatic lane changing, and parking assistance. It can respond to traffic lights and stop signs, making it a more comprehensive driver-assistance tool than we have seen or been used to. One of Tesla's unique advantages is its ability to leverage data from its global fleet of vehicles. Every mile driven by a Tesla contributes to the training of its neural networks, enabling the system to learn and improve over time. This iterative process enhances safety and performance, bringing Tesla closer to achieving fully autonomous driving.

While Autopilot is currently classified as a Level 2 autonomous system (requiring driver supervision), Tesla's long-term goal is to achieve Level 5 autonomy – where vehicles operate without human intervention. Achieving this will require overcoming technical, regulatory, and ethical challenges, some of which we discuss in further chapters. And could significantly disrupt long-established industries like haulage, public transport, courier services, and even aviation. The impact of removing the human driver extends well beyond engineering as it affects economies, jobs, and the social fabric of how we move.

The success of Tesla has spurred other automakers to invest heavily in AI-driven technologies. From General Motors' Super Cruise to Waymo's autonomous vehicles, investment in AI-powered innovation is reshaping the future of transportation.

Education: Personalising learning experiences

And finally, AI is reshaping education – making learning more personalised than ever – both in the classroom and online. It can track a student's progress, pinpoint areas where they're struggling, and adjust lessons to meet their needs. Beyond helping teachers fine-tune their approach, AI also powers the new adaptive learning platforms, which allow students to learn at their own pace, making education more flexible, accessible, and tailored to each individual.

- ***Adaptive learning platforms*:** AI systems can adjust lesson plans and assessments based on a student's progress and comprehension. Tools like Carnegie Learning provide customised learning paths to address specific challenges.
- ***Language learning*:** Apps like Duolingo language learning use AI to create engaging, interactive lessons that adapt to a user's proficiency level, ensuring steady progress.

- ***Accessibility tools:*** New solutions are using real-time transcription and text-to-speech converters, enabling students with different abilities to access educational content more easily.
- ***Administrative efficiency:*** AI automates admin tasks – like grading and attendance tracking – allowing educators to focus on teaching.

I'm a huge advocate of online learning – utilising it extensively in both my professional and personal learning – and Coursera and edX are two of the main providers I've used. Both use AI to recommend courses, track progress, and provide personalised feedback. Their platforms democratise access to education, enabling learners worldwide to acquire new skills – in their own time and location – on a huge range of topics that were previously not so accessible.

Traditional classroom models face challenges like large class sizes, varying student abilities, and limited resources. These issues can make it difficult to provide personalised attention to every student. Traditional online education platforms, while scalable, can lack the interactivity and adaptability of in-person instruction. AI offers a solution by enabling customised learning experiences at scale. Algorithms analyse student performance – on practice problems, quizzes, and assignments – to identify strengths and weaknesses. Based on this analysis, the platforms suggest tailored learning paths, ensuring students focus on areas where they need the most improvement.

Natural language processing (NLP) also enables platforms to offer multilingual support. This opens the door for students from diverse linguistic backgrounds to access content in their preferred language. The learning centres that are linked to professional qualifications and courses can also equip educators with dashboards that provide insights into class progress. Teachers can now see which students are excelling, who needs additional help, and which topics require a revisit.

What we've uncovered here is just a small snippet of how AI's transformative impact is spanning industries – bringing innovation and improving efficiency in ways once thought impossible. From diagnosing diseases to optimising supply chains, AI is solving some of our most complex challenges and creating value across sectors. As these applications continue to evolve, they will redefine the boundaries of what we can achieve, meaning AI will remain a catalyst for progress for years to come. While each sector faces its own unique challenges, specific common themes are starting to emerge.

While each sector faces its own unique challenges, some common themes are starting to emerge; scalability, enabling organisations to grow in ways previously impossible; efficiency, reducing costs and increasing productivity through automation and better decision-making; and customer-centric innovation, using AI to personalise experiences and anticipate user needs.

The road ahead

The success of these AI applications underscores the importance of continued investment in infrastructure and ethical frameworks. As AI technologies mature, they will expand what is possible across industries, further blurring the lines between human expertise and machine intelligence. However, it is the industries implementing these solutions that need to consider the human interaction element, to avoid replacing a system for the sake of it without any real benefit.

Looking across these examples, you can start to see how AI is being applied to drive innovation and create lasting impact within organisations. The key is understanding where it can genuinely solve problems in your own business and industry.

Challenges in deploying AI today

While Artificial Intelligence is demonstrating huge potential across industries, its deployment is not without hurdles and challenges which span human uptake and interaction, technical, ethical, and regulatory domains, often requiring a multidisciplinary approach to be addressed effectively. These topics are introduced briefly here to provide a solid starting point – many of them are explored in more depth later in the book, where we build on these foundations.

Navigating the age of surveillance

The cornerstone of AI's capabilities lies in its access to massive datasets, but this reliance on data raises profound privacy concerns. AI systems collect, process, and analyse personal information from various sources, including social media, e-commerce platforms, and IoT devices. While this data fuels AI's accuracy and adaptability, it also creates risks related to misuse, unauthorised access, and surveillance. I address this further in Chapter 4, which provides a more detailed examination of ethics and data protection.

Regulatory and legal challenges

The rapid advancement of AI has outpaced the development of comprehensive regulatory frameworks. This regulatory gap creates uncertainty for businesses and raises concerns about the ethical and legal implications of AI deployment. Countries vary widely in their approach to AI governance, and this disparity complicates cross-border operations for multinational organisations. Governments are working to introduce strong regulations to tackle data privacy concerns – but the scope is so vast that covering every aspect is a challenge.

Laws like the European Union's General Data Protection Regulation (EUGDPR), the UK's GDPR, the California Consumer Privacy Act (CCPA), and the EU's AI Act (EUAI) are all major steps towards giving individuals more control over their data. These regulations require organisations to be transparent about how they collect, store, and process information – often imposing strict rules on data localisation, anonymisation, and user consent. While these safeguards are essential, they can also be resource-intensive for businesses. For multinational companies, navigating conflicting regulations across different regions adds yet another layer of complexity.

Technological solutions, like federated learning and differential privacy, offer promising ways to address privacy concerns. Federated learning allows AI models to learn from decentralised data without transferring it to a central server, reducing the risk of breaches. Differential privacy introduces noise into datasets, protecting individual identities while preserving analytical value.

However, AI models are only as good as the data on which they are trained, and biased datasets can lead to discriminatory outcomes. Bias in AI manifests in various forms, from facial recognition systems that misidentify individuals from certain demographic groups to hiring algorithms that inadvertently favour one gender over another.

AI-generated content raises questions about intellectual property rights. Who owns the copyright to an image created by a generative AI model? Resolving these issues requires ongoing updates to existing legal frameworks.

Determining liability for AI-driven decisions is a complex and challenging task. In the case of an autonomous vehicle accident, should the responsibility lie with the

manufacturer, the software developer, or the user? Clear legal standards are needed to address these scenarios.
Biased AI systems can exacerbate inequalities in areas like criminal justice, hiring, and lending. For instance, predictive policing algorithms have been criticised for disproportionately targeting marginalised communities, raising ethical and legal concerns.
To combat bias, we need to understand how to prioritise diversity in data collection and AI development teams. Techniques like fairness-aware machine learning and adversarial debiasing are gaining traction. Additionally, third-party audits and XAI frameworks can help identify and rectify biases in deployed systems.

The financial and environmental burden

As we've discussed before, deploying AI systems has only really been possible with new and substantial computational resources, making it a costly endeavour. Training large models like the latest GPT models involves thousands of GPUs running for weeks, consuming vast amounts of electricity and water. These costs pose challenges for small and medium-sized enterprises, raising concerns about the environmental impact of AI.
High-performance hardware, cloud computing services, and skilled personnel are major cost drivers in AI deployment. For startups and SMEs, these expenses can slow innovation and limit competition in the AI market.
AI's energy consumption contributes to carbon emissions, particularly in regions reliant on non-renewable energy

sources. Training a single deep learning model can generate as much carbon as 5 cars over their lifetimes. This environmental cost has sparked calls for more sustainable AI practices.

Researchers are developing more efficient algorithms to reduce the computational overhead of AI training and inference. By shifting computations from centralised servers to edge devices, latency is decreased, and energy consumption is reduced, contributing to more sustainable AI deployment. Data centres powered by renewable energy sources are increasingly being built to minimise AI's carbon footprint. While these facilities are growing in number, their construction and operation require significant resources, posing challenges to fully sustainable deployment at scale.

The black box problem

Many AI models, particularly deep learning systems, operate as "black boxes", making it difficult to understand how they arrive at their decisions. This lack of interpretability undermines trust and complicates the detection of errors or biases.

XAI aims to make AI systems more interpretable by providing insights into their decision-making processes. Techniques such as LIME (Local Interpretable Model-agnostic Explanations) and SHAP (SHapley Additive exPlanations) are widely used to enhance transparency. So, when looking at AI systems and considering your move, take a moment to really understand how your AI will be interpreted, and whether you can justify its decisions.

Workforce displacement and reskilling

AI's automation capabilities have sparked fears of job displacement – particularly in sectors like manufacturing, logistics, and customer service. Although AI creates new opportunities, the transition requires significant reskilling and workforce adaptation. The jobs of tomorrow have yet to be discovered or even created. Reskilling is challenging without knowing what you need to learn, especially when the required skills are changing rapidly. Jobs involving repetitive or routine tasks, like assembly line work and data entry, are most vulnerable to automation. However, even highly skilled roles in fields like law and medicine face changes as AI systems augment human expertise.
As part of any AI deployment or integration into your business, you need to understand how you will invest in reskilling programmes to equip workers with the skills required for AI-driven industries. Emphasising digital literacy, creativity, and problem-solving will help people thrive in an AI-enhanced workforce.

We've now covered many topics, from the birth and evolution of AI and those first pioneers, to what and how it's being used today, along with a brief discussion about the potential pitfalls and some of the challenges you may face.

So how do you go about implementing AI into *your* business? Let's explore what you need to think about and understand to bring AI into your organisation successfully.

Chapter 3: Implementing AI in your business

The journey from understanding AI's potential to successfully implementing it is far from straightforward. While many organisations are eager to adopt AI, they often face challenges such as unclear goals, inadequate resources, and resistance to change. One of the biggest challenges you will face is identifying the use case. AI is regularly implemented in a manner of "*a solution looking for a problem*"! You need to clearly identify a problem you want to solve and then understand whether AI is the right tool to do the job.

This chapter bridges the gap between AI theory and practical application, guiding you through actionable steps to integrate AI into your business operations. Unlike earlier chapters that focus on the evolution and transformative power of AI across various industries, this section is designed to provide you with a hands-on framework. Whether you're just beginning to explore AI or looking to scale existing initiatives, this chapter equips you with the tools and strategies needed for successful implementation.

We'll cover the essential steps of assessing your company's readiness for AI, crafting a strategic roadmap, and fostering a culture of collaboration and innovation.

You'll also learn how to choose the right technologies, optimise data usage, and measure the impact of AI projects. By the end of the chapter, you'll have a clear, actionable plan to take AI from concept to reality in your business.

AI is not a one-size-fits-all solution. Its success depends on aligning its implementation with your organisation's unique goals, resources, and challenges. As you explore the following sections, remember that successful AI adoption is not just about technology; it's about ethics, people, strategy, and execution.

Building an AI strategic plan

In the next two sections, we'll discuss both strategy and tactical delivery. The strategic plan provides the "why" and the "what": Why AI is important for your organisation's future, and what overarching goals you hope to achieve. The tactical plan delivers the "how" and the "when": How the AI initiatives will be executed, and when key milestones and deliverables will be completed. Having both plans in place helps you maintain a clear vision while ensuring that the practical steps needed to achieve that vision are well-coordinated and achievable.

A word of warning, though – many organisational leaders fall into a common trap: skipping the strategic planning phase and asking their IT teams to "just deliver AI". They recognise the buzzword of AI, understand that it promises greater value and productivity, but lack clarity on its true capabilities or how it aligns with their business objectives.

Without a strategic plan, AI initiatives risk becoming a series of disconnected projects that fail to deliver meaningful results – wasting both time and resources. The key area of concern when building out your strategy is problem identification. Find the problem you are trying to solve and truly understand if and how AI will achieve it. A strategic plan, combined with effective leadership, is crucial to avoid this pitfall. AI adoption isn't just an IT project; it's a transformative effort that impacts the entire company. You need to be clear about who will take ownership of defining the vision, identifying priorities, and communicating the "why" behind AI's role in the future. By doing so, they can provide the direction needed to guide tactical delivery, ensuring that every initiative serves a cohesive purpose and drives measurable outcomes. This person should be a senior figure and leader within your business to ensure it's not just lip service, but a genuine strategy. Only with this strong strategic foundation can you move forward confidently.

Strategic plan: The long-term vision

At its heart, a strategic AI plan sets the direction by defining how AI will address key business challenges or opportunities. A healthcare organisation might leverage AI for improving patient outcomes through predictive diagnostics, while a retail business might focus on enhancing customer experiences with personalised recommendations. By aligning AI initiatives with mission-critical objectives, you can ensure that resources are invested where they deliver the most impact. Also, remember that not all AI initiatives are created equal, and a well-thought-out strategy focuses on those that align with both short-term wins and long-term ambitions. For instance, pilot projects that demonstrate quick results, like automating repetitive tasks, can build momentum and support for more complex and transformative initiatives. This balance of incremental improvements and ambitious goals allows you to scale AI sustainably.

A strong strategy also creates a foundation for integration across the business. This involves planning for scalable infrastructure, fostering collaboration between departments, and embedding AI into the organisational culture. Long-term success requires more than deploying technology; it demands leadership buy-in, ethical guidelines for AI use – and, most importantly, a workforce that is prepared to engage with AI tools effectively.

Ultimately, a strategic plan for AI ensures that adoption is not just reactive or experimental but part of a forward-thinking vision. By setting clear priorities, aligning with business goals, and building for scalability, you can deliver sustainable value and long-term success.

I've identified what I believe are the 5 key components to defining your AI strategy.

1. **Business vision alignment**

Aligning AI with your overarching business mission is essential to ensure its adoption delivers meaningful and measurable value. AI must serve as a strategic enabler,

directly addressing your goals and challenges, rather than just a tool adopted by tech teams. This alignment ensures that AI is not an abstract project but a practical tool for achieving your specific business objectives.
Leadership plays a pivotal role in recognising the potential and capability of AI in achieving alignment. Effective leaders must not only understand AI's abilities but also champion its adoption as a driver of growth and innovation. This involves communicating a clear vision of how AI will support the mission, securing stakeholder buy-in, and fostering confidence in its benefits. Without these two alignments and leadership commitment, AI initiatives risk becoming disjointed experiments rather than cohesive, strategic efforts. By defining a clear vision for AI that directly aligns with your business goals, you can ensure that resources are directed toward impactful, mission-critical projects.

2. Scalability

Scalability is a cornerstone of a successful AI strategy. It enables you to expand the use of AI across departments and regions in a controlled and sustainable manner. Implementing AI begins with pilot projects in a specific area – providing a low-risk opportunity to test the technology's effectiveness. Once these pilot projects have demonstrated success, they can be gradually expanded to other areas, ensuring that lessons learned in the initial phase are applied to subsequent deployments.

Investing in scalable infrastructure is also critical to supporting the growth of your AI deployments. Cloud-based systems offer flexibility and cost efficiency, enabling businesses to scale computational resources as needed without significant upfront investment. Modular platforms can also be beneficial, as they allow for incremental upgrades and customisation to meet evolving business requirements. By planning for scalability from the outset, you can avoid bottlenecks that hinder growth and ensure that your projects remain sustainable, cost-effective, and adaptable as adoption grows.

3. Ethics and governance

Ethics and governance must be integral to your AI strategy – providing the framework to manage risks and ensure accountability is paramount. Your systems must be designed and deployed with ethical considerations in mind, addressing challenges like data bias, privacy concerns, and regulatory compliance. Any algorithms trained on biased data can produce discriminatory outcomes, undermining trust and fairness in the system. We cover ethics in more detail in the next chapter. However, it's important to recognise that structures are in place to oversee the development and deployment of AI systems, ensuring they comply with legal and ethical standards. Make sure you establish governance teams or committees to review your AI models and put safeguards in place to mitigate potential risks. You can also conduct regular audits and publish clear documentation of your AI processes, to further enhance accountability, helping to maintain public and/or stakeholder trust.

4. Cultural transformation

Successfully implementing AI requires a cultural shift within your organisation, where your teams see AI not as a threat but as a tool for empowerment. This begins with your leadership team. Having buy-in and clear communication about AI's role in supporting – rather than replacing – human capabilities is fundamental. To achieve this cultural transformation, it is essential to promote continuous learning and upskilling. Providing training programmes, workshops, and certifications helps your team develop the skills to work confidently alongside AI technologies. If you foster a culture of collaboration and growth, you can ensure that your workforce is prepared to thrive in an AI-driven future.

I can't overstate this point – implementing AI successfully isn't just an IT project; it requires buy-in and collaboration across all departments. The 'Cross-Department Collaboration Playbook' downloadable from www.benjaminrowe.com *provides practical strategies to align teams, and facilitate effective communication, ensuring that everyone works together to maximise the value of AI.*

5. Innovation portfolio

Your project portfolio shouldn't just include AI initiatives; it should be viewed as part of a broader innovation portfolio – balancing high-risk, transformative projects with low-risk, incremental improvements. Transformative projects – such as developing a proprietary AI model for market prediction – can drive significant competitive advantages but can require substantial investment and carry greater uncertainty. On the other hand, incremental improvements, like automating routine tasks, provide quick wins and can build momentum for more ambitious efforts.

Regularly reviewing and adapting the project portfolio ensures it remains aligned with market trends and goals. As our technology evolves, some projects may need to pivot or be reprioritised, while new opportunities may emerge. By treating AI as a dynamic component of a broader innovation strategy, you can understand and maintain flexibility and continue to drive value from your improvement initiatives.

Key takeaway

Crafting a strong AI strategy is the foundation for everything that follows. Without it, tactical efforts risk becoming fragmented or reactive, and misaligned with your goals. Skipping this step is like setting off on a car journey without a map; you may be moving, but with no clear direction, destination, or timeframe for when you will arrive. A strategy led by leadership ensures your AI initiatives align with the business objectives and by establishing a clear vision you can prioritise goals, and embedding scalability and ethics. Only once this roadmap is complete should you proceed to your tactical execution – where the strategy is transformed into coordinated action and measurable results.

Remember:
AI is not a solution looking for a problem. Find the problems you want to solve – and make sure AI is the correct tool for the job

A well-defined roadmap is essential for AI implementation. The 'AI Roadmap Builder', available for download from www.benjaminrowe.com, *helps break down your AI journey into clear phases, from identifying opportunities to scaling successful projects.*

Building an AI tactical plan

Now that you've given your strategic plan some thought and set the vision, you can turn your attention to the tactical plan and outline the steps required to achieve it. This plan translates your high-level strategy into specific tasks, deliverables, and timelines - giving your teams clear direction.

Breaking the process into manageable phases helps you avoid taking on overly ambitious projects without sufficient preparation. Each phase builds on the previous one, creating a logical progression that allows your team to learn, adapt, and refine their approach along the way. This phased approach minimises risk and ensures that resources - whether time, budget, or talent - are allocated efficiently and aligned with strategic priorities.

A tactical roadmap also provides a framework for engaging your stakeholders across the organisation. By defining clear milestones and deliverables, it facilitates communication and collaboration between departments, ensuring that everyone understands their role in the AI journey. Whether you're piloting a chatbot for customer service or scaling predictive analytics across multiple business units, a roadmap keeps your entire organisation moving in the same direction - focused on achieving measurable results. Ultimately, your roadmap transforms the abstract potential of the project into actionable steps, turning uncertainty into a clear path toward innovation and success. Think of it as a commitment to your strategy that delivers thoughtful implementation and real value.

Phases of implementation

The phases of implementation provide a structured approach for everyone to adopt and scale AI within a business or team. They typically include research and exploration – where potential use cases are identified and feasibility is assessed; pilot projects – which test AI solutions on a small scale to validate their effectiveness and refine approaches; and full-scale deployment – where successful pilots are expanded across the identified user base with proper integration and monitoring.
Let's break down these phases to understand what they are, why they are necessary, and what you need to consider.

- ***Research and exploration***

Begin by thoroughly understanding your identified use cases and the specific challenges or opportunities they aim to address – like automating repetitive tasks or enhancing customer engagement. This ensures the project scope remains focused on achieving the right goals with tangible business value. Conduct feasibility studies and undertake a gap analysis to evaluate whether the necessary data, infrastructure, and expertise are in place to support the initiative effectively. Engaging stakeholders early is essential. Their diverse perspectives can refine the approach – and bring new insights not considered previously – while fostering alignment and securing buy-in across the organisation by involving everyone.

- ***Pilot projects***

Testing AI solutions on a small scale through pilot projects is a critical step in the implementation process. These projects enable teams to verify the effectiveness of AI in addressing specific business needs, like improving response times with chatbots or enhancing supply chain efficiency with predictive analytics. Pilots also provide an opportunity to identify challenges while refining approaches, and measure success using metrics like cost savings or customer satisfaction. By starting with manageable, low-risk initiatives, you can build confidence and establish a foundation for broader adoption.

- ***Full-scale deployment and monitoring***

Once pilot projects have demonstrated success, the next step is to expand these solutions across the departments and business through full-scale deployment. This involves integrating AI systems into existing workflows – ensuring they align with operational processes – and scaling them to cover broader use cases. Ensuring you have adequate training and support for your employees is crucial at this stage to facilitate adoption and maximise the technology's impact. Monitoring your project outcomes is equally essential; ongoing performance evaluation ensures the AI continues to deliver value, and regular updates or retraining can address changing needs or data patterns. Full-scale deployment, coupled with robust monitoring, ensures your system implementation remains a dynamic and effective tool for long-term business success.

- ***Timelines and resource allocation***

Establishing realistic timelines – and allocating resources effectively – will be essential to the success of any AI initiative. Clear timelines help manage expectations and ensure that each phase of the project progresses without unnecessary delays. Data preparation might take several weeks, while pilot testing could extend over a quarter. Simultaneously, resources – whether financial, technological, or human – must be allocated strategically to focus on priority projects that align with your organisational goals. In balancing timelines with available resources, you ensure that AI projects remain practical, achievable, and sustainable, paving the way for long-term success.

Prioritising use cases

AI offers a vast array of potential applications; however, not all use cases provide the same level of value or feasibility for every organisation. Choosing where to focus your efforts is important to ensure your AI initiatives yield meaningful results – without overextending resources or introducing unnecessary complexity.

Prioritising the right projects involves identifying use cases that align with your strategic goals, have a measurable impact, and are practical to implement with existing resources. High-priority projects often address pressing challenges, such as improving customer satisfaction or streamlining operational inefficiencies, while offering clear, quantifiable benefits. Equally important is evaluating feasibility, where projects that rely on high-quality, readily available data or require minimal changes to existing infrastructure are better starting points than those that require significant overhauls or untested approaches.

If you focus on initiatives that deliver maximum impact with minimal complexity, you can build momentum, trust, and confidence in AI capabilities. This not only minimises your risk but also ensures that resources – whether time, budget, or talent – are used effectively while helping your teams see results quickly and build the skills and confidence needed to mature their use of AI. A well-prioritised approach sets the stage for long-term success, enabling you to expand your AI efforts with a strong foundation of proven results.

Here's a quick rundown of the selection criteria to help you review them more easily.

High impact

Select use cases that significantly enhance operations or improve customer satisfaction.

- Automating customer service with AI chatbots to reduce response times.
- Using predictive analytics to forecast sales trends and optimise inventory.

Low complexity and cost

Start with projects that are relatively simple to implement and have a low financial barrier.

- Automating repetitive back-office tasks like invoice processing.
- Deploying AI to analyse customer feedback for insights.

Data availability

- Choose projects where sufficient, high-quality data is available to train AI models effectively.
- Highlight projects where data can be accessed easily, securely, and quickly with minimal impact on operational infrastructure.

Business case

Once your tactical roadmap is outlined, the next step is to consolidate it into a formal business case. This document brings together the problem statement, proposed solution, expected outcomes, costs, and resource requirements, thereby securing stakeholder buy-in. A clear business case helps decision-makers understand both the strategic intent and the operational realities, making it easier to approve funding and commit the necessary support so you can move forward with confidence.

Budgeting and resource allocation

AI implementation requires a robust budgeting process to ensure financial sustainability while delivering measurable value. Beyond the initial purchase of tools or software, you must consider a range of additional costs, including operational expenses, scaling needs, and talent development. A tactical approach focuses on breaking these costs down into actionable phases aligned with project milestones – enabling better resource management, adaptability, and cash flow planning.

These costs would also have to cover pilots, which require targeted resources to test specific use cases. Operational expenses, such as retraining models and monitoring system performance, represent ongoing commitments that ensure AI systems remain accurate and effective.

Additionally, scaling successful AI initiatives – whether you are expanding infrastructure, integrating new workflows, or upgrading tools – requires careful planning to avoid overwhelming resources.

The leaders in your business must decide whether to hire specialists for immediate expertise or invest in upskilling existing staff for long-term capacity building – or somewhere in between. Talent acquisition and training are crucial components of any project but are especially relevant when implementing AI solutions. There is potential to mix and have flexible solutions, like combining internal teams with external consultants. This can help address short-term needs while building internal expertise, giving your teams knowledge and confidence.

However, ensure that you build in handover time, so the knowledge doesn't walk out the door at the end of the engagement.

To justify this expense, calculating return on investment will be essential. Use the 'ROI Calculator for AI Projects' to estimate costs, benefits, and overall return." This includes measuring factors like cost savings, time saved, efficiency gains, and revenue increases generated by AI initiatives. Even a simple £20 per month AI tool can be cost-neutral if it saves just one hour of an employee's time – time that would otherwise be a direct cost to the business. By adopting a tactical approach to your budget, you can manage expenses dynamically, align expenditures with outcomes, and ensure AI projects deliver tangible value. Of course, not all AI projects will deliver cost savings in terms of financial bottom-line benefits. Customer service satisfaction, for instance, is difficult to measure on a balance sheet, yet it can dramatically enhance the customer experience.

Return on investment is a critical part of any AI initiative. Use the 'ROI Calculator worksheet' to estimate costs, expected benefits, and return. This worksheet, available for download at www.benjaminrowe.com, helps you quantify value and ensure your AI investments are aligned to measurable business outcomes.

Setting realistic timelines

Effective time planning is important for keeping AI projects on track and ensuring that each phase of implementation progresses smoothly. Without a clear timeline, projects can face delays, resource bottlenecks, or scope creep, and your teams can easily be distracted by some fanciful new piece of tech or idea. A structured approach to time planning ensures that each phase of your tactical plan is realistic and achievable.

Break projects into manageable phases

- Divide the implementation process into distinct stages, like research, pilot testing, and deployment. Assign specific timeframes to each phase based on its complexity and requirements.
- Data preparation might take 2–4 weeks, while training and testing AI models could span several months; however, AI could even be used to assist in this to speed up the process.

Set milestones and deadlines

- Establish clear milestones to track progress, such as "Complete data collection by the end of month 1" or "Deploy pilot chatbot by month 3".
- Deadlines should balance urgency with feasibility – ensuring teams have enough time to complete tasks without compromising quality.

Account for buffer time

- Include contingency time in your planning to account for unexpected challenges, like delays in data preparation or technical integration issues.
- Buffer time prevents minor delays from cascading into larger disruptions.

Synchronise with organisational goals

- Align project timelines with broader business objectives, for example, launching an AI-driven customer service tool before the holiday season to handle increased demand.
- Ensure that timeframes are coordinated across departments to avoid conflicts or resource overlaps.

Monitor and adjust timelines

- Regularly review timelines and progress. Use project management tools to track tasks and dependencies, identifying delays early.
- Be flexible enough to adjust timeframes if unforeseen obstacles arise, while maintaining focus on overarching goals.

Time planning is the backbone of any successful project execution – AI projects are no exception. By breaking the project into phases, setting realistic deadlines, and allowing for flexibility, you can keep your AI initiatives on schedule and maintain momentum. Whether using

Waterfall, Agile, or any other project methodology, keeping on top of your progress and timelines is a key challenge to overcome, especially when new tech and ideas come into play along with knowns and unknowns about data and dependencies.

Key takeaways

Implementing AI effectively requires more than just investing in technology; it demands a structured, strategic approach to ensure success. By focusing on clear planning, prioritising impactful projects, and allocating resources judiciously, you can navigate the complexities while minimising your risks. A well-executed strategy helps avoid pitfalls – like overspending, misaligned goals, or stalled projects – while a clear roadmap provides a structured plan to guide you through the phased implementation process, ensuring each step aligns with your business objectives.

Prioritising high-value use cases ensures resources are focused on projects that deliver the greatest impact with the least complexity. At the same time, careful budgeting and resource management allow you to balance costs with measurable benefits, ensuring financial sustainability. Together, these steps create a solid foundation for achieving tangible, long-term results from AI initiatives. Ensure that you communicate both the strategic objectives and the tactical plan to all stakeholders – so everyone is aware of what's happening, when, and how – for maximum delivery.

That's a quick overview of the steps. Let's unpack these topics in broader detail with a step-by-step guide to help you create your own plans.

Assessing readiness for AI adoption

Here's a big question... Are you actually ready for AI? And some minor but equally essential follow-ups: Do you need AI? Do your employees want AI? Do your customers?
The first step is identifying the specific challenges or opportunities where AI can add value. AI is not a solution in search of a problem – because it works best when applied to clearly defined business needs with measurable outcomes. This means taking a close look at your organisation's current operations, pain points, and growth objectives to determine where AI can have the most meaningful impact.

Understanding business needs

Let's get to grips with what you want to achieve. To begin, identify areas where inefficiencies or limitations hinder performance. For example, are manual processes slowing down team productivity? Do your teams struggle to make sense of vast amounts of data? Are there frequent errors or inconsistencies in specific workflows? AI can be particularly effective in addressing straightforward, repetitive tasks and improving decision-making through the analysis of formatted data, as well as automating time-consuming processes.

Next, identify opportunities to enhance existing capabilities or introduce entirely new solutions. AI might enable your business to predict customer behaviour, personalise marketing strategies, or optimise supply chains. Think about how AI could help you innovate your products, increase your competitiveness in your specific market, or improve customer satisfaction. In recent studies by KPMG, many metrics of AI adoption have focused on productivity over profitability, so don't go reaching for the calculator just yet!

By framing your business needs in terms of a specific problem to solve or opportunities to seize, you can ensure that your AI initiatives are purposeful and impactful. This clarity not only improves the likelihood of success but also helps secure buy-in from stakeholders who need to see the tangible benefits of AI investment.

Here are some questions you can ask yourself:

- Are paper or process inefficiencies slowing down our operations?
- Are there repetitive tasks that could be automated?
- Do we struggle with making data-driven decisions due to a lack of insights or analysis?
- How could predictive analytics improve our sales forecasting?
- Could chatbots enhance our customer service experience?

- Are there ways to use AI to gain a competitive edge?

Now that you have some ideas, I've put together a 5-step guide in the *'AI use case assessment template'* to help you identify specific areas for your own use. Adjust the requirements for your area of concern but be self-critical and really hone the scope. The goal is to avoid falling into the trap of trying to get AI to "fix" problems that don't exist. Check out this and all the other toolkits at www.benjaminrowe.com where a copy of this is available to help you through the process.

1. **Start:** Begin by asking the fundamental question: *What is the primary goal or challenge our business wants to address?*

- Your objective will probably fall under one of two broad categories: **operational efficiency** or **strategic growth**.

2. **If it's operational efficiency:**

- Focus on identifying inefficiencies, like repetitive manual tasks, process delays, or high costs.
- Next, assess the potential for automation or AI-powered tools to streamline these processes.

3. **If it's strategic growth:**

- Define key objectives like improving customer engagement, enhancing product offerings, or entering new markets.

- Explore AI solutions that align with these objectives, such as recommendation systems or predictive analytics.

4. **Outcomes:**

   - For **operational efficiency**, the outcome is improved productivity and reduced costs.
   - For **strategic growth**, the outcome is enhanced customer satisfaction, innovation, and revenue growth.

5. **Final step:**

- Ensure the identified problem or goal is measurable and define clear success metrics. This enables your business to effectively evaluate the impact of AI and adjust its strategies as needed.

Evaluating current resources

Once you've identified potential areas where AI can add value, the next step is to assess whether your organisation is prepared to adopt and implement these technologies effectively. This involves taking a close look at your resources, infrastructure, and the skills within your team to ensure a solid foundation for AI integration. Without this readiness, even the most promising AI initiatives can falter.

Data resources

AI thrives on data; it's the essential fuel that powers algorithms, trains models, and enables systems to generate insights and make predictions. Without high-quality data, even the most advanced AI tools cannot deliver accurate or meaningful results. Data forms the backbone of all AI applications – from customer segmentation and recommendation systems to predictive analytics and process automation. To ensure your organisation is ready to start a project and for it to become effective, it's essential to evaluate your data readiness across several dimensions, including its volume, quality, accessibility, and relevance to your business needs.

- ***Volume***: Do you have enough data to train AI models effectively? Small datasets may require augmentation or external sources.
- ***Quality***: Is your data clean, accurate, and consistent? Poor-quality data can lead to unreliable AI predictions.
- ***Accessibility***: Are your data systems siloed, or do you have integrated data platforms? Seamless access to data across departments is essential for AI success.

If your data resources are lacking, consider starting with smaller AI applications that rely on simpler datasets while simultaneously investing in data collection, integration, and cleaning processes.

Data is the lifeblood of AI. Assess your organisation's data infrastructure, quality, and accessibility with the 'Data Readiness Audit Tool'. This worksheet, available for download at www.benjaminrowe.com, *ensures your foundation is strong before embarking on AI initiatives.*

Technological infrastructure

Any AI implementation requires robust tech to support and ensure systems can handle the demands of training models, running algorithms, and processing all this lovely data you have accumulated efficiently. This support includes critical components like computing power, storage, and specialised software tools designed for AI applications. Without the right infrastructure, AI projects can face performance bottlenecks, scalability issues, or even complete failure. When evaluating your technological readiness, consider key factors like the adequacy of your current systems, the scalability of your infrastructure to handle growing AI demands, and the availability of tools tailored to your specific use cases. Additionally, explore whether on-premises solutions, cloud-based platforms, or hybrid models best suit your organisation's needs and budget. This comprehensive assessment lays the foundation for successful AI deployment and long-term sustainability.

- ***Current systems***: Are your IT systems modern enough to support AI, or do they need upgrades?

- ***Scalability***: Can your infrastructure handle the growing demands of AI applications as they expand?
- ***Cloud solutions***: If in-house systems are insufficient, can cloud-based platforms like AWS, Microsoft Azure, or Google Cloud provide the needed scalability and tools?

Investing in scalable and flexible infrastructure ensures your organisation can handle the technical demands of AI projects now and in the future.

Workforce skills

Your team's ability to manage and work alongside AI technologies is key to the success of any implementation. Even the most sophisticated AI systems require knowledgeable individuals to guide their development, deployment, and maintenance. Begin by evaluating the current skill levels within your organisation – particularly in areas such as data analytics, machine learning, and AI-specific tools. Do team members have the technical expertise to interpret AI-generated insights and apply them to business decisions effectively? If not, identify those opportunities to bridge the skills gap through online courses, or certifications.

Consider creating dedicated roles within your organisation, like data scientists, AI engineers, or machine learning specialists, who can spearhead your AI projects. These roles act as the linchpin between AI technologies

and business objectives, ensuring alignment and optimal outcomes. Also, assess the adaptability of your broader workforce. Can team members learn to use AI-driven tools in their day-to-day tasks, for example, by automating repetitive work or generating reports?
You will also need to ensure that employees feel supported and informed about AI's role in enhancing – and not replacing – their contributions. Clear communication, hands-on training, and ongoing support can help mitigate resistance and create a workforce that is confident and prepared to work alongside these new AI technologies. Building this capability within your team ensures smoother adoption and unlocks the full potential of AI as a transformative tool for your business.

- ***Existing skills***: Do your employees have expertise in data science, machine learning, or AI application management?
- ***Upskilling needs***: If there are gaps, can you invest in training programmes to upskill your workforce? Online courses, workshops, and partnerships with academic institutions can help bridge the skills gap.
- ***Dedicated roles***: Consider hiring specialists like data scientists, machine learning engineers, or AI consultants to lead your initiatives.

By ensuring your workforce is equipped with the necessary skills, you create a supportive environment for AI adoption.

Leadership and stakeholder alignment

Your AI initiatives will require strong leadership and buy-in from all your key stakeholders to ensure their success and alignment with the broader organisational goals. Effective leadership will be vital for setting a clear vision for AI adoption, communicating its potential benefits, and addressing any concerns or resistance that may arise within the organisation.

Review whether your leadership team has a solid understanding of AI's capabilities and limitations. Do they have a clear vision of how AI can address business challenges, improve efficiency, or drive innovation? If not, consider providing educational resources or workshops to build this foundational knowledge. The simple decision flow below can help you determine your team's current standing and identify the next steps you need to take.

AI leadership readiness: quick decision flow

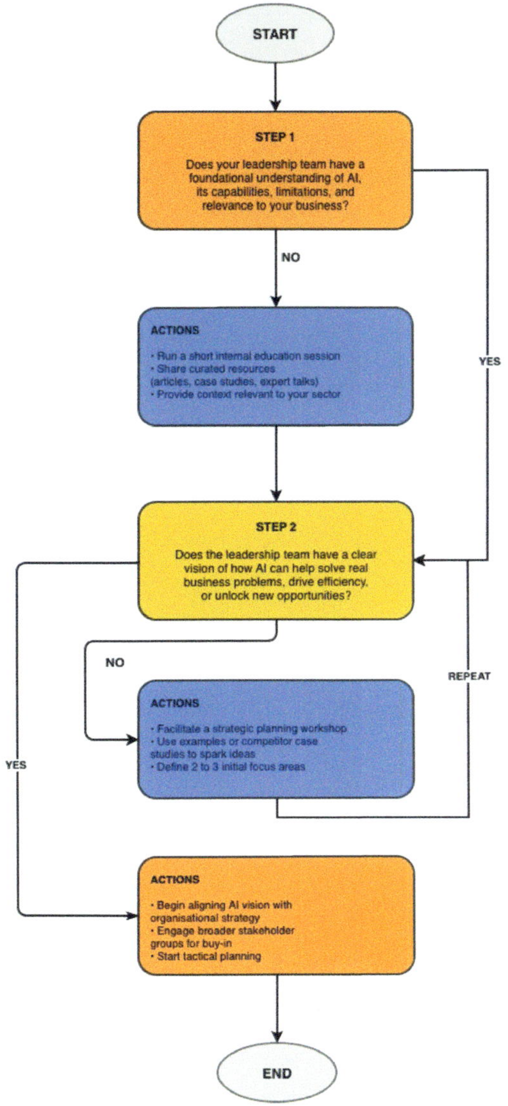

Stakeholder support is equally important. Evaluate the willingness of executives, department heads, and other key decision-makers to invest the necessary time, budget, and resources into AI projects. Are they aligned with the goals and expected outcomes? Misalignment can lead to fragmented efforts, inadequate funding, or even project failure.

Leaders must also be able to articulate how AI aligns with your business objectives, its potential return on investment, and how it will impact employees and workflows. This clarity will not only foster trust but will also ensure that AI adoption is seen as a strategic priority rather than a disruptive force.

Finally, assess whether your organisation has a framework for measuring the success of leadership-driven AI initiatives. Clear accountability, regular progress reviews, and the ability to pivot when challenges arise are essential for maintaining momentum and ensuring long-term success.

- ***Vision***: Do your leaders understand AI's potential and have a clear vision for its role in the organisation?
- ***Support***: Are stakeholders willing to invest time, resources, and funding in AI projects?
- ***Communication***: Ensure leaders and teams are aligned on AI's objectives and outcomes to avoid confusion and resistance.

Strong leadership and stakeholder buy-in lay the foundation for all successful AI projects.

AI Stakeholder Communication Guide
Communicating the value and implications of AI to stakeholders is a significant success factor. Use the 'AI Stakeholder Communication Guide' to structure your conversations, ensuring alignment with organisational goals and addressing concerns from both technical and non-technical audiences. This can be downloaded at www.benjaminrowe.com

Budget and resources

AI projects vary significantly in cost depending on their scope, business sector, and complexity. Make sure you evaluate your financial readiness:

- ***Initial investment*:** Do you have the budget for tools, talent, and training?
- ***Long-term costs*:** Consider ongoing maintenance, retraining models, and scaling successful projects – AI is not a "set and forget" technology.
- ***Return on investment (ROI)*:** Identify potential gains from AI initiatives to justify costs and secure funding.

Start by estimating the initial investment. This typically includes the cost of acquiring AI tools and platforms, upgrading existing infrastructure, and potentially hiring external consultants or experts to guide the implementation. Custom AI solutions, like developing proprietary machine learning models, may be more expensive than off-the-shelf tools designed for general use.

An overlooked aspect of AI adoption is its ongoing costs. Many companies believe that once they have implemented the solution, the process is complete. However, there are ongoing expenses involved in maintaining and updating AI systems, retraining models as data evolves, and scaling successful projects across the organisation. For cloud-based AI platforms, subscription fees or pay-as-you-go models will also contribute to your long-term costs. Ensure your budget includes these recurring expenses.
Next, it's time to evaluate the potential return on investment! AI can drive significant value by reducing costs and opening new revenue streams. For example, an AI-driven recommendation system may increase e-commerce sales, or a predictive maintenance solution may reduce equipment repair costs. Conduct a cost-benefit analysis to estimate the financial impact of your AI initiatives, ensuring that anticipated benefits outweigh the potential associated expenses. However, be cautious: consider this from a long-term perspective. Your first project might *not* break even right away, but further implementations could open doors later on.
Finally, assess your organisation's capacity for resource allocation. Are funds readily available for AI projects, or will you need to secure additional budget approvals? Presenting a clear financial plan with measurable outcomes can help secure the necessary support. By thoroughly evaluating your financial readiness, you can lay the groundwork for AI projects that are both impactful and economically sustainable.

Remember, setting **SMART** goals always helps to achieve project success:

- ***S**pecific*: Clearly define what you want AI to achieve.
  Example: "Reduce customer response time by 50% using AI-powered chatbots."
- ***M**easurable*: Establish metrics to evaluate success.
  Example: "Increase sales by 10% through AI-driven product recommendations."
- ***A**chievable*: Ensure the goal is realistic given your resources and timeframe.
- ***R**elevant*: Align AI efforts with your organisation's broader objectives.
- ***T**ime-bound*: Set deadlines for achieving milestones.

Managing risks is important for the sustainable deployment of AI. The 'AI Project Risk Mitigation Plan' downloadable from www.benjaminrowe.com helps identify potential pitfalls early and provides strategies to address them effectively.

Balancing the triple constraint in projects

The Triple Constraint Triangle is a practical constraint in project management. This model highlights the trade-offs between three variables: time, cost, and quality/scope. It should be considered at the beginning of any new project including AI.

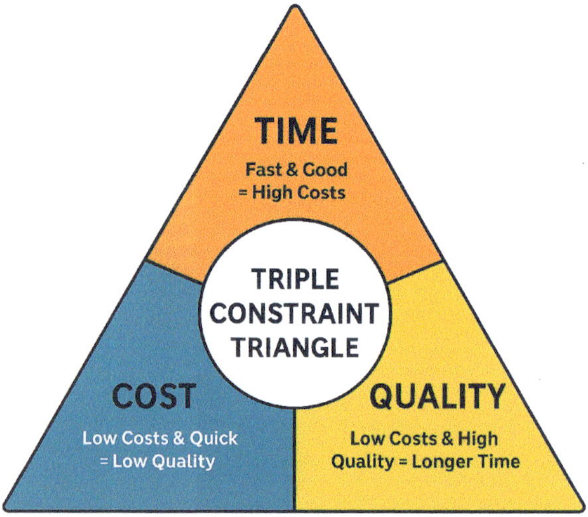

- ***Time:*** Faster project delivery may increase costs or reduce quality if resources are stretched.

A common mistake is rushing to deploy quickly to gain a competitive edge or meet urgent demands. However, prioritising speed may mean sacrificing quality or incurring increased costs by allocating additional resources, such as hiring external consultants or investing in expedited tools and infrastructure

- ***Cost:*** Minimising costs can extend timelines or limit the scope and quality of the AI solution.

Cost encompasses the financial resources required to complete the project, including tools, infrastructure, talent acquisition, and ongoing maintenance. Minimising costs is a common priority, but it will likely extend project timelines and/or reduce the quality of deliverables if resources are spread too thin.

- ***Quality/Scope:*** Delivering high-quality results may require more time and budget to refine and deploy effectively.

Quality refers to the standards of the deliverables and how well the AI project meets its intended goals. Scope defines the extent of the project's objectives, for example the complexity of AI models or the breadth of use cases. Delivering a high-quality AI solution with a broad scope requires more time and resources for refinement, testing, and deployment.

The reality is that you can typically optimise for two of these factors, but not all three:

- *If you prioritise time and cost,* quality or scope will suffer. Rushing an AI chatbot project with a limited budget may result in a tool that lacks essential features.
- *If you prioritise time and quality,* costs will increase. You may want to allocate additional funds to hire specialists or invest in faster

computing infrastructure to achieve high standards.

- *If you prioritise cost and quality*, the project will take longer. Building a robust AI-driven recommendation engine on a tight budget might require stretching the timeline to accommodate limited resources.

Practical exercise: AI readiness checklist

To help you assess your readiness, use this 5-point checklist:

1. Have you identified clear business problems or opportunities for AI?
2. Is your data readily available, clean, and relevant?
3. Do you have the infrastructure (or access to cloud platforms) to support your AI project?
4. Are your teams skilled or prepared for AI adoption, or do you have a plan for upskilling or hiring?
5. Have you defined specific, measurable goals for your AI initiatives?

If you answered "no" to any of these questions, start by addressing those gaps before moving to the implementation phase. AI adoption is a journey, and laying a strong foundation is critical to its success.

Use the toolkits and worksheets available for download from www.benjaminrowe.com to support your AI journey.

Collaborating across teams

Fostering a culture of innovation and engagement

Change can be difficult and frightening – especially when we anticipate new technology. This uncertainty can be unsettling. As we've just discussed, for AI adoption to succeed, it must be supported by strong leadership and a collaborative organisational culture. Without strong leadership buy-in, AI initiatives risk becoming fragmented or being labelled as just another business project and ignored, with your teams viewing them as a passing trend rather than an opportunity. Leaders who fail to champion its potential can inadvertently create resistance, and employees may see AI as a threat to their roles rather than the tool for improvement and empowerment that leaders want it to be. AI adoption will also require teams across departments to work together seamlessly.

Unlike traditional IT projects, AI initiatives can span multiple functions to share data and insights to drive business decisions. Without this early alignment and a clear understanding of how AI outputs will be used, your teams could become siloed, leading to miscommunication and inefficient decision-making. A lack of collaboration undermines the very essence of AI's purpose: to provide a holistic view of business challenges and opportunities. This resistance can stall projects before they even begin and waste valuable time and resources.

There needs to be a culture of innovation where collaboration is prioritised, and all your teams feel empowered to engage without feeling alienated by AI. Promoting literacy through workshops, open communication, and discussion will be essential to demystifying the technology and building trust. When teams understand how AI can automate repetitive tasks - enhance their roles - and help with decision-making, they are more likely to embrace its integration.

Ultimately, failing to invest in a culture of innovation and cross-departmental collaboration jeopardises the success of AI projects and can alienate employees. As a leader, you must recognise that AI adoption is not just a technology initiative, but a transformative effort that requires unity, understanding, and a shared commitment across the organisation.

Choosing the right technologies

Selecting the right technology is a decision that lays the foundation for successful implementation and long-term scalability. With numerous tools, platforms, and vendors available, you need to carefully evaluate options to ensure alignment with your business needs, current tech stack, ease of integration, and adaptability to future challenges. This section explores the criteria for selecting AI platforms, partnering with vendors, and building in-house expertise to create a robust and sustainable AI ecosystem.

Selecting AI tools and platforms

You should prioritise technologies that align with your specific use cases and can grow with your needs over time. There are some key criteria for evaluating AI platforms that you can build on.

***Scalability*:**

- AI projects should start small and then expand rapidly once the technology has been demonstrated - valued - and use cases evolve, and successes are scaled out across departments. A scalable platform ensures that initial investments continue to deliver value without the need for costly replacements or upgrades. Cloud-based platforms like AWS AI, Google Cloud AI, and Microsoft Azure AI provide flexible and scalable solutions that can accommodate increasing demands.

***Ease of integration*:**

- AI platforms should integrate seamlessly with existing systems and workflows to minimise disruption. Compatibility with enterprise software, databases, and APIs is essential to ensure smooth data exchange and operational efficiency. For example, platforms like TensorFlow and PyTorch* are widely compatible with other tools, making them ideal for organisations with complex IT ecosystems.

Vendor support and community resources:

- Strong vendor support is vital for troubleshooting, updates, and guidance during implementation. Platforms with active user communities and open-source resources, like TensorFlow and scikit-learn, provide access to a wealth of knowledge and tools that can accelerate development and problem-solving.

*Popular AI platforms include TensorFlow (an open-source framework ideal for custom AI solutions), AWS AI (offering pre-built tools and cloud services), Microsoft Azure AI (known for its integration with Microsoft's enterprise products), and Google Cloud AI (renowned for its machine learning and analytics capabilities). Evaluating these options based on scalability, integration, and support ensures that the selected technology aligns with both your current and future organisational needs.

Partnering with vendors

While in-house AI development offers long-term independence, many organisations choose to partner with vendors or consultants to accelerate their AI journey, especially during the initial stages. Choosing the right vendor is a strategic decision that can determine the success of your AI initiative.

References and case studies:

- Evaluate potential vendors by reviewing their past work and expertise with the chosen technology stack. Case studies that demonstrate successful implementations of similar use cases – regardless of the industry – provide valuable insights into the vendor's capabilities and reliability. A vendor with substantial experience in deploying AI-powered predictive analytics using the same technology platform your organisation plans to adopt should be considered, even if their previous work was in a different sector. This approach ensures that technical proficiency and solution delivery are prioritised over narrowly focused industry experience.

Alignment with business goals:

- A successful partnership requires the vendor's approach to align with your organisation's objectives. Vendors should demonstrate an understanding of your unique challenges and offer customised solutions rather than generic implementations.

Flexibility and collaboration:

- Look for vendors who are willing to work closely with internal teams, share knowledge, and adapt their solutions as the project evolves. A collaborative approach ensures that your organisation retains control and can build internal expertise over time.

Engaging vendors can provide access to specialised skills and deployment, thereby reducing the learning curve for your organisation to adopt AI. However, you should ensure that partnerships do not lead to over-reliance, especially for long-term initiatives.

Selecting the right AI vendor is a pivotal decision. The 'AI Vendor Evaluation Scorecard' downloadable at www.benjaminrowe.com, provides a structured approach to comparing vendors based on scalability, integration, and support capabilities.

Building in-house expertise

Bringing AI expertise in-house allows you to maintain control, drive innovation, and adapt solutions to your unique needs. While external vendors can accelerate the early adoption of AI, relying solely on third-party providers limits any business's ability to evolve independently and maximise the long-term potential of AI. Developing an internal team of skilled professionals ensures that your AI initiatives remain aligned with your goals and can respond quickly to changes in strategy or market dynamics.

***Hiring AI talent*:**

- Recruiting skilled AI professionals – such as data scientists, machine learning engineers, and AI project managers – is a significant step to ensure you are building internal expertise. These roles bring specialised knowledge that allows you to design, deploy, and refine your AI systems effectively.

***Retraining existing staff*:**

- Upskilling employees is a cost-effective and strong strategy for building, developing, and retaining great teams. Many professionals who are already familiar with organisational processes can develop their AI toolset or manage AI projects. Platforms like Coursera, DataCamp, and company-led workshops offer accessible options for education.

***Long-term scalability and independence*:**

- An in-house AI team enables you to respond quickly to evolving needs, test new ideas, and scale projects without external vendor or budget constraints. Internal teams can refine AI models as data evolves or adapt existing solutions to new use cases, ensuring continuous value creation.

Having in-house experts means your teams can design and refine the AI systems with complete autonomy. These specialists will gain a deep understanding of your business processes, data, and goals, enabling them to create solutions tailored to your specific needs and challenges.

These internal teams can experiment with custom AI models and implement enhancements without calling on external help.

Over time, this capability will reduce dependency on external vendors and build your team's confidence to experiment with new ideas and ensure that intellectual property – for example proprietary AI models or algorithms – remains within your business.
The 'AI Literacy Starter Pack', downloadable from www.benjaminrowe.com, is designed to introduce employees to key concepts, demystify AI technologies, and spark their curiosity.

Monitoring and optimising AI projects

Monitoring tech projects is not a one-time activity, and AI projects are no exception; they are an ongoing process that ensures your systems perform as expected and meet the goals you set at the beginning. Regular evaluation helps identify issues like data drift – where the data being processed changes over time, potentially reducing the accuracy of your AI models. To put that in perspective, a predictive analytics tool for customer behaviour may lose effectiveness if consumer trends shift dramatically; suddenly, your AI tool is no longer delivering your results, and without monitoring, you won't know why.

Defining KPIs

Key performance indicators can be a handy tool for monitoring. But their value lies in more than just measurement; they must drive action. There's no point in defining a measurement if you aren't going to do anything with the outcome. When defining KPIs for AI initiatives, ensure each metric provides clear, actionable insights that lead to informed decisions and improvements. Without this focus, monitoring becomes an exercise in reporting rather than optimisation.

To establish good actionable KPIs, start by aligning them with the specific business goals you outlined in your original project plan. An AI-powered recommendation engine might track metrics like click-through or conversion rates. If these indicators fall below expectations, the action could involve retraining the algorithm with updated data, refining the recommendation logic, or integrating user feedback to improve relevance. Similarly, a fraud detection system might measure the rate of false positives versus the actual number of fraud cases. A spike in false positives could trigger a review of the model's thresholds or data quality to recalibrate performance.

Monitoring KPIs should also include a process for translating insights into operational adjustments by assigning responsibility for reviewing the metrics and implementing changes to cross-functional teams, ensuring collaboration between technical staff and business stakeholders. Suppose a KPI reveals that customer satisfaction scores have dropped after deploying an AI chatbot. In that case, the action might involve refining the chatbot's conversational capabilities, adding escalation options to live agents, or adjusting its use cases.

Finally, ensure KPIs are dynamic and regularly reviewed. As your business priorities or market conditions change, the relevance of specific metrics may shift, which can be an overlooked aspect of the process. Many businesses implement KPIs but fail to review them. And years down the line, they are still looking at the same reports without actionable insights, "Because that's the way we've always done it." Regular reviews of both the KPIs themselves and their corresponding actions ensure the monitoring framework evolves alongside your goals. This approach transforms your KPI tracking from passive measurement to an active driver of continuous improvement and value creation.

Here are 10 examples of KPIs that *could* be used to guide the effective monitoring and evaluation of AI projects. These are suggestions – you will review your own use cases and develop KPIs to suit your specific needs.

1. ***Accuracy***: Measure the percentage of correct predictions or outputs made by an AI model. For example, in a fraud detection system, this would be the proportion of correctly identified fraudulent transactions.
2. ***Precision and recall***: Precision measures the proportion of actual positive results among all positive predictions, while recall measures the proportion of true positives identified out of all actual positives. These are useful in systems like medical diagnosis or spam filtering, where the balance between identifying true cases and avoiding false positives is vital.

3. ***Uptime and availability*:** Tracks the reliability of an AI system, ensuring it's as operational and accessible as needed. This is especially important for customer-facing AI solutions like chatbots or virtual assistants.
4. ***Model training time*:** Measures the time it takes to train a model with new data. Faster training times can indicate more efficient workflows or systems, while longer times might signal bottlenecks that need addressing or data sets that are too large and cumbersome to manage.
5. ***Latency*:** Refers to the time taken by an AI system to produce a result after receiving input. Low latency is particularly important for real-time systems like autonomous vehicles or live customer support tools.
6. ***Adoption rate*:** Measures how widely and effectively an AI solution is being used across the organisation. A high adoption rate indicates that employees or users find the tool valuable and easy to integrate into their workflows.
7. ***Return on investment (ROI)*:** Tracks the financial gains or cost savings generated by an AI project relative to its implementation and operational costs.
8. ***Customer satisfaction (CSAT)*:** Measures the impact of AI on customer experience, such as through surveys or feedback scores. Evaluating

how well a recommendation engine or chatbot meets customer needs.

9. ***False positive/false negative rates*:** Tracks the errors in an AI model's predictions. In fraud detection or medical diagnosis, reducing these rates is essential for improving overall system reliability and user trust.
10. ***Data drift metrics*:** Monitor how the input data distribution changes over time compared to the data used during training. Significant drift can indicate the need to retrain the model to maintain performance.

Selecting the right KPIs depends on the specific goals and use cases of the AI project in question, as well as who will be reviewing and reporting on the metrics. For instance, your technical team may want a different set of metrics to your C-suite.

Iterative improvement

AI systems thrive on iterative improvement, a process that leverages feedback loops to refine and optimise performance over time. Unlike static systems, AI models are dynamic, requiring regular updates to adapt to changing data patterns, your evolving business needs, and potentially any external conditions.

Feedback loops enable continuous learning by using insights from system outputs and user interactions to inform refinements of the system. For example, a recommendation engine can analyse customer behaviours, such as clicks and purchases – to adjust its suggestions dynamically – and fraud detection systems can incorporate newly identified fraudulent patterns into their models, improving accuracy and reducing false positives.

To support iterative improvement, consider employing tools and frameworks designed for monitoring AI model performance. Platforms like MLflow, Amazon SageMaker, or Azure Machine Learning provide dashboards and automated alerts to track metrics like accuracy, precision, and recall in real-time. These tools enable teams to identify performance issues, for example data drift or reduced model accuracy, early in the process, minimising disruptions to operations.

As your data evolves, retraining your AI models ensures the system adapts to new patterns or contexts. A good real-world example of this is a sentiment analysis tool used for social media monitoring, which may need periodic updates to recognise new slang or cultural nuances. Make sure that a retraining schedule is included, supported by robust monitoring and feedback mechanisms, to ensure that the models not only maintain their performance but also become increasingly effective over time.

Scaling successful projects

The connection between scaling and monitoring lies in the need for consistent oversight and adaptation as your model and projects grow in scope. As the solutions expand beyond the pilot phase, monitoring them ensures that they maintain their performance across new, more complex environments. An AI model that performed well in a single department may encounter challenges when deployed in other areas with different workflows or data structures. This is where monitoring plays a vital role in identifying these inconsistencies and providing insights for necessary adjustments.

Scaling often introduces complexities not encountered during the pilot phase – as new variables, increased data volumes, or additional user feedback can impact performance. Monitoring systems track these changes over time allowing you to highlight bottlenecks like slower processing times or reduced accuracy, so it can be addressed proactively. As AI is applied to broader use cases; retraining these models may become necessary to adapt to changing conditions or your expanded datasets. The monitoring tools you use will facilitate this process by identifying areas where the model's predictions are less reliable and can guide targeted improvements.

As you scale your AI systems across your departments or regions, the monitoring you use ensures alignment with your organisational goals. By tracking performance metrics across all deployment areas, your project and business leadership can confirm that the expanded rollout continues to deliver value and supports strategic objectives. Without monitoring, the scaling efforts risk introducing inefficiencies, degraded performance, or misaligned priorities. Monitoring serves as the backbone of a successful scaling strategy, ensuring that growth amplifies AI's benefits rather than diminishing its effectiveness.

Overcoming common challenges

Managing expectations in AI projects

AI right now is surrounded by hype. Business leaders are expecting quick, transformative results, but that's not always the case, especially in complex businesses. Achieving meaningful outcomes requires time, effort, and gradual progress. Only by setting realistic timelines and goals can you avoid the common mistake of over-promising and under-delivering.

One key to managing expectations is recognising that an AI implementation is a phased process. A pilot programme that focuses on automating a single repetitive task – such as an invoice processing solution – is a great way to demonstrate its potential before scaling the idea to other departments. Promising sweeping changes too quickly can lead to frustration among teams and leaders if results take longer than anticipated or if unforeseen challenges arise. Instead, we need to understand the practicalities of implementation and communicate the iterative nature of AI projects, emphasising that quick wins during the pilot phase – while laying the groundwork for broader transformation – is the process we need to follow, which will be more effective in the long run.

Another common mistake is expecting AI to deliver flawless results immediately. Remember that all AI models rely on data, and their performance improves over time with refinement and retraining. You should prepare stakeholders for this learning curve by framing early iterations as opportunities for improvement rather than final products, and by training staff to identify errors and problems. **A key point to remember is that the first deployment is always the worst; it will improve over time, but in sensitive environments, it's crucial to have people closely monitoring outcomes and ready to intervene if needed.**

Addressing resistance to change

Resistance to change is a common hurdle in any project, especially those in the tech sector, and this is no different for AI adoption. Employees may fear that new technology and automation will render their roles obsolete. If you address these concerns head-on and reassure your teams, you can start to build the essential trust and foster a culture where AI is viewed as an opportunity rather than a threat. The key factor should be clearly articulating how AI aligns with your organisation's goals and enhances employee roles.

AI excels at automating repetitive, time-consuming tasks, freeing your teams to focus on more strategic, creative, or customer-facing activities. For example, a marketing team might use AI tools to handle data analysis, allowing them to spend more time crafting impactful campaigns.

However, this should be clearly communicated before any AI deployment, so everyone understands how their roles will change and can prepare to adapt and adjust accordingly.

Offering excellent training programmes and workshops before deployment can also help develop the skills needed to work alongside AI technologies, empowering everyone to stay relevant in an evolving workplace.

Involving your teams in the implementation process can further reduce resistance. Seeking their input on use cases or inviting them to participate in pilot projects demonstrates that you value their expertise and input. When people see themselves as collaborators in adoption, they are more likely to embrace the changes it brings. By emphasising AI as a tool for empowerment rather than replacement, and providing resources to support through the transition, you can create a positive, inclusive environment where AI is welcomed as a partner and stand a much higher chance of success.

Navigating ethical and regulatory issues

Ethical and regulatory challenges are among the most complex aspects of AI adoption, necessitating a careful balance between innovation and responsibility for businesses. Just because you *can* do something doesn't always mean you *should*.

Ensuring compliance with data protection regulations, such as the GDPR or the EUAI, is a critical starting point. Practical steps can include conducting regular audits of

data handling practices, ensuring transparency in the use of data, and obtaining explicit consent from individuals as required. Appointing a Data Protection Officer (DPO) to oversee compliance efforts can really help businesses stay aligned with these ever-evolving legal requirements.
Ethical dilemmas intersect with regulatory issues, particularly in areas like data privacy, bias, and accountability. Dealing with these issues involves embedding fairness and accountability into your AI development by diversifying datasets and implementing governance frameworks to monitor ethical considerations. These frameworks are essential for ensuring that AI tools produce equitable and trustworthy results.
This is a significant topic, and therefore, we need to explore the broader implications of AI ethics in greater depth. We are only just at the start of the major uptake of AI, and many of the laws and ethical ideals have yet to be written or challenged. That's where it's up to you to determine the future. You will need to discuss topics like bias mitigation, data protection, accountability in decision-making, and the long-term societal impact of AI. Let's explore these topics further in the next chapter, where I've provided a comprehensive, yet not exhaustive, practical guide to navigating these challenges responsibly.

Conclusion

Implementing AI in your business is a journey that requires both vision and discipline. It's essential to define the critical steps to ensure success, starting with setting a clear strategic direction that aligns with your organisation's goals. A strong strategy provides the foundation for translating high-level objectives into actionable, tactical steps, ensuring that every initiative serves a broader purpose. Without this alignment, AI risks becoming a disconnected set of experiments rather than a transformative force.

I'm a strong supporter of businesses starting small to showcase AI's potential without overwhelming resources or introducing unnecessary risks. Pilot projects will allow you to test use cases, refine approaches, and demonstrate value on a manageable scale. These early successes will provide proof of concept and build on momentum and confidence for larger-scale rollouts. Importantly, AI is not a one-and-done effort; it thrives on iterative improvement. Monitoring performance, integrating feedback, and retraining models to ensure that AI systems remain accurate, effective, and aligned with your changing business needs.

I've also tried to underscore the importance of fostering a collaborative culture, addressing resistance to change, and prioritising ethical considerations. AI is not just an IT initiative; it requires the buy-in and cooperation of leaders, employees, teams, and stakeholders across your organisation. Transparency, communication, and upskilling are essential to building trust and empowering teams to embrace AI as an enabler rather than a disruptor. As you move forward, remember that AI is more than just a technology; it's a tool that, when implemented correctly, is capable of unlocking new opportunities, driving the ever-important efficiency, and enhancing your decision-making options. Success lies not in rushing to adopt the latest tools and tech, but in approaching AI strategically, tactically, and iteratively, like any other business project. By starting with a strong strategy, learning through experimentation, and remaining committed to continuous improvement, you can harness AI's potential to innovate, grow, and succeed.

Chapter 4: Ethics and challenges

As Artificial Intelligence becomes increasingly integrated into society, it introduces profound ethical dilemmas and challenges that demand thoughtful solutions. These issues span data protection, algorithmic bias, accountability, AI hallucination, and regulatory complexities. Ensuring that AI benefits all of humanity requires proactive efforts from AI professionals, business leaders, governments, researchers, and civil society. We will explore the key ethical concerns and challenges posed by AI, examining real-world examples, regulatory landscapes, and the roles of various stakeholders in shaping a responsible AI future. AI systems operate on large datasets, raising issues around privacy, security, and fairness. As these systems influence critical decisions in areas such as healthcare, finance, and law enforcement, they risk amplifying biases or making opaque decisions that affect human lives. Beyond individual use cases, the integration of AI into society raises broader questions about its long-term implications. How can we ensure that AI-driven automation does not exacerbate inequality? Who should be held accountable when AI systems fail? At the same time, the regulatory landscape is undergoing rapid evolution. Legislation like the EUAI is introducing strict governance frameworks around AI use, with hefty penalties for non-compliance. Other countries are expected to follow, making it essential for businesses operating across borders to stay informed about varying AI regulations.

Ethical dilemmas

AI systems are inherently shaped by the data used to train them, and if that data contains biases, whether due to historical inequities, cultural stereotypes, or systemic disparities, those biases can be perpetuated or even amplified by the AI. These biases can lead to unfair outcomes, for example, marginalising underrepresented groups or reinforcing societal inequalities.

- ***Facial recognition***: Studies have shown that facial recognition systems regularly perform less accurately for individuals from underrepresented groups – particularly women and people of colour. This has led to wrongful arrests and heightened scrutiny on the use of these technologies by law enforcement.
- ***Hiring algorithms***: In one case, an AI recruitment tool developed by a major tech company was found to favour male candidates because its training data predominantly reflected historical hiring practices that favoured men.
- ***Inaccurate data sets***: If, for example, the wrong postcode was included on an application form, this could result in a person not being able to get credit

until the error was rectified, and adverse effects on their credit score.

So how can we address these biased systems? What steps can we take, and when should humans intervene? Organisations must adopt a proactive, multi-faceted approach that combines technical solutions with human oversight. Bias in AI does not arise solely from flawed algorithms; it is often rooted in the data used to train these systems. By addressing the problem at its source and throughout the development lifecycle, businesses can create AI systems that are fairer – more inclusive – and less likely to produce harmful outcomes.
The first step is ensuring that datasets are representative and diverse. Many AI systems are trained on datasets that reflect existing societal imbalances or exclude certain demographics. Regularly reviewing AI models for unintended consequences allows teams to identify and address discriminatory behaviour before deployment. Techniques like fairness metrics, counterfactual testing, and adversarial simulations can help uncover hidden biases and improve algorithmic decision-making. These audits should be conducted throughout the AI lifecycle, from development to deployment in real-world applications.
While AI excels at processing vast amounts of data, it lacks the context and ethical judgement that humans bring to decision-making. GDPR requires human review if the decision being made is "legal or similarly significant", and therefore, the check must have meaningful input if

challenged. Combining this human review with AI outputs can act as a safeguard, ensuring that decisions align with organisational values and societal expectations.
We must not lose sight of the fact that strong human oversight is always required. You can reduce bias in AI systems and build trust in their use, but there will always be opportunities for them to be flawed, and therefore, they will need intervention. These steps are not just technical necessities; they are ethical imperatives for creating AI systems that serve everyone impartially.

Privacy and surveillance

The rise of AI-powered surveillance technologies has fundamentally changed the way governments, businesses, and individuals monitor and analyse human activity. While these systems enhance security and operational efficiency, they also raise profound ethical questions about privacy, human rights, and the potential for misuse. A key dilemma is whether individuals have the right to live their lives without constant monitoring. In many public spaces, surveillance is considered an inherent part of modern life, with the assumption that being in a public area implies permission to be filmed. However, this norm is increasingly challenged as AI systems amplify the scope and scale of surveillance.
Where does society draw the line between legitimate public safety measures and invasive government monitoring? Surveillance intended to prevent crime or

improve public safety can easily drift into overreach when used to monitor everyday behaviour without justification. This raises fundamental questions about human rights: Should individuals have a say in how they are monitored, or does public safety override personal consent? Balancing these competing priorities is critical as AI surveillance becomes more pervasive.

Applications of AI in surveillance

Governments frequently use AI technologies such as facial recognition, behaviour analysis, and licence plate tracking to monitor public spaces. These systems can enhance safety by identifying suspects or managing large events. For instance, facial recognition has been effectively used to identify wanted individuals at crowded public gatherings. Yet these benefits come with risks. In authoritarian regimes, such technologies can be employed to suppress dissent, monitor activists, and maintain control. Even in democratic societies, unchecked surveillance can erode trust and disproportionately impact marginalised groups, raising concerns about fairness and accountability.

In the private sector, AI-powered surveillance is increasingly prevalent in retail, marketing, and e-commerce. Companies monitor consumer behaviour through browsing patterns, purchase histories, and even physical movements in stores. These insights enable businesses to personalise services and predict customer needs, creating more tailored experiences. However, these practices frequently occur without explicit consent, raising concerns about informed choice and data ownership. The commodification of personal data highlights the trade-offs between convenience and privacy, particularly when consumer data is sold to third parties or used to manipulate purchasing decisions.

Balancing security and privacy

Organisations and governments must disclose how data is collected, stored, and used, providing clear and accessible explanations to the public. Regulations like the GDPR and the EUAI specifically mandate transparency and require organisations to obtain explicit consent for data collection. Compliance with such standards not only protects privacy but also builds trust by demonstrating accountability. By removing personally identifiable information from datasets, organisations can extract valuable insights without compromising individual identities. Traffic cameras, for example, might analyse anonymised data to optimise city planning without tracking specific drivers. Similarly, retailers can study purchasing trends while protecting customer identities. Encryption and secure storage of data enhance these efforts, ensuring that sensitive information remains inaccessible to unauthorised parties.

Policymakers, technologists, and communities must engage in open discussions about what constitutes acceptable use of these technologies. Such dialogue can

help align surveillance practices with societal values, ensuring responsible design and implementation.
When surveillance systems fail – or are misused – clear governance structures are needed to assign responsibility and implement corrective actions. Independent oversight committees, transparent reporting, and strict regulatory frameworks can help ensure that these technologies are used ethically and effectively.

The future of AI surveillance

As AI surveillance continues to evolve, its impact on society will depend largely on how it is governed and deployed. Striking a balance between security and privacy, with an open public dialogue, and integrating ethical principles into the development and use of these systems are steps toward ensuring that surveillance serves the greater good. The line between public safety and unwarranted intrusion is a delicate one, and maintaining this balance will require vigilance, transparency, and a commitment to protecting fundamental rights.
Ultimately, AI surveillance has the potential to enhance security and drive innovation, but only if its implementation respects individual freedoms and societal values. We need to address these challenges head-on, so we can harness the power of AI responsibly, creating a future where technology serves humanity without compromising the rights that define us.

Data protection & regulatory challenges

The rise of Artificial Intelligence presents significant regulatory challenges, particularly in the realm of data protection and privacy. As AI systems become increasingly embedded in business operations and public life, the need to ensure compliance with evolving data protection laws has never been greater. Regulations such as the GDPR and CCPA have established crucial benchmarks for protecting consumer data. However, enforcing these regulations in an AI-driven world is complicated by the scale, complexity, and global nature of data flows.

One of the fundamental questions in the AI era is: Who owns the data? AI systems rely on vast quantities of data to function effectively, but much of this data originates from individuals, which raises concerns about both privacy and intellectual property. So, when a consumer interacts with a digital assistant, the system collects and analyses data to personalise responses. The individual, the organisation collecting it, the company storing it, or the company that developed the AI tool. Understanding ownership matters because the storage or collecting company owning the data could then use it to train their own algorithms for their benefit. Clarifying ownership rights helps resolve disputes and ensuring fair use. However, it must be classified at the point of data entry, which is a major concern since most chat systems do not specify data ownership.

From personal details to complex behavioural patterns, data is the lifeblood that powers predictive models, decision-making algorithms, and automated systems. However, this reliance also presents significant vulnerabilities. Breaches, misuse, or inadequate safeguards can lead to devastating consequences – including financial losses, reputational damage, and ethical violations. Data protection is not just a technical requirement but a core responsibility for everyone.
In a world where trust is as valuable as innovation, the handling of sensitive data has a direct impact on a company's credibility. Customers, employees, and stakeholders expect their information to be managed securely and ethically. Without proper data protection, AI systems risk becoming unreliable, producing biased outcomes, or functioning sub optimally due to contaminated datasets. By treating data protection as foundational, businesses can mitigate risks and enhance the overall effectiveness of their AI initiatives.

Compliance challenges with global regulations

The global regulatory landscape adds complexity to data protection, particularly for businesses that operate across multiple jurisdictions. The GDPR and the CCPA impose stringent requirements on how data is collected, stored, and processed. While these regulations aim to protect consumer rights, their unique provisions and scope will create challenges for organisations. A key difficulty is in

the variation between laws. GDPR, for example, mandates explicit consent and data minimisation principles, while the CCPA focuses on consumer rights, such as the ability to opt out of data sales.
The GDPR's "right to explanation" compels organisations to disclose how AI systems use personal data. While this promotes accountability, it can also risk exposing proprietary technology, creating a delicate balance between compliance and protecting intellectual property. Additionally, the dynamic nature of regulatory environments means that organisations must constantly monitor legislative changes, adding ongoing complexity. These differences require organisations to develop region-specific strategies to remain compliant. The restrictions on cross-border data transfers introduce additional hurdles, necessitating the use of mechanisms like Standard Contractual Clauses (SCCs) or Binding Corporate Rules (BCRs) to move data between countries legally.

Algorithmic transparency

Data protection laws require you to explain how you use personal information, but AI systems, especially those based on deep learning, are inherently complex. Algorithms usually operate as "black boxes", making it difficult to understand how they process data or reach decisions. Ensuring compliance with transparency requirements is, therefore, a major challenge. If an AI system denies a loan application, the affected individual has a right to understand the reasoning behind the decision. You must find ways to make these explanations accessible while maintaining proprietary protections for the technology.

Developing global standards for AI governance would streamline compliance and reduce barriers for multinational organisations, but this is a long and complex process.

Existing regulations were not designed with AI's unique characteristics in mind. AI-specific legislation is necessary to address challenges like algorithm accountability, bias mitigation, and the dynamic nature of decision-making processes. For example, laws could require organisations to conduct algorithmic audits, ensuring that AI systems are free from discriminatory practices and comply with ethical standards.

The EUAI is the closest piece of legislation currently available, having officially come into force in August 2024. However, its application is being phased in gradually, with only some provisions currently active, and full implementation taking place over time. For now, the Act provides a strong starting point, but much still rests on each company's own ethical and moral compass when it comes to the deployment of AI. This should be treated with the utmost respect; without it, mistrust in AI will become a significant concern.

Strategies for securing data

To safeguard the data that fuels AI systems, you must adopt an approach where encryption is the cornerstone of data security, ensuring that sensitive information remains inaccessible to unauthorised individuals. Modern encryption standards, such as AES-256, protect data both at rest and in transit, making it virtually impossible for malicious actors to interpret stolen information. Implementing end-to-end encryption adds an additional layer of security by keeping data protected throughout its entire lifecycle.

Access control mechanisms support data security by aligning access rights with job responsibilities, limiting exposure to only those who require specific information to perform their roles effectively. Multi-factor authentication further strengthens this approach, adding a layer of verification that makes it harder for intrusions to occur. Meanwhile, anonymisation techniques – like data masking and differential privacy – provide an effective way to protect sensitive information during the training of AI models. These methods preserve the utility of datasets while removing personally identifiable details, ensuring privacy remains intact.

Segmentation of data is another effective measure, particularly for companies managing large datasets. By categorising information based on sensitivity, you can tailor security measures to different segments. This limits the impact of potential breaches, as attackers would only access a subset of the data rather than the entire repository. Regular security audits further bolster this framework, helping identify vulnerabilities and ensuring compliance with ever-evolving security standards.

Emerging best practices like zero-trust architectures

In response to growing threats, zero-trust architectures (ZTAs) have emerged as a leading framework for securing modern systems, including those powered by AI. Unlike traditional perimeter-based security models, ZTAs operate on the principle of "never trust, always verify". This philosophy assumes that every interaction, regardless of origin, must be verified before granting access. ZTAs incorporate several key practices that enhance security for AI systems.

By enforcing the principle of least privilege, organisations ensure that users and systems can only access the data and resources necessary for their roles. Continuous verification mechanisms evaluate access permissions based on real-time behaviour and contextual information, minimising the risk of unauthorised activities. Additionally, micro-segmentation divides networks into smaller zones, preventing threats from spreading laterally in the event of a breach. By encrypting all communications, ZTAs further protect sensitive information from interception and unauthorised access.

For AI systems, these practices are particularly beneficial. The complex, distributed nature of AI environments often involves multiple stakeholders, data sources, and infrastructure components. A zero-trust approach reduces vulnerabilities across this ecosystem, aligning with regulatory requirements while providing scalability and flexibility.

Practical implications for businesses using AI

The adoption of AI brings important responsibilities for protecting data. For businesses, it's not just about following regulations, but also about building trust and maintaining secure operations. Employees are usually the first line of defence against cyber threats, so they need regular training on data protection and compliance requirements.

Strong governance is key. Any project involving AI and personal information should be done in consultation with a data protection team, and a data protection impact assessment (DPIA) should be conducted.

Assigning clear roles, such as a Data Protection Officer (DPO), ensures someone is always accountable for keeping data safe and meeting legal standards.

Beyond securing data, companies must focus on being transparent, fair, and respectful of privacy. Using tools that explain how AI decisions are made and avoid bias can help build trust. Secure AI platforms with built-in compliance features can also simplify these efforts.

Finally, AI systems need regular check-ups. Since they are constantly updated with new data, routine risk assessments can help find and fix vulnerabilities, ensuring long-term security.

Areas for further exploration

While these strategies address many aspects of data protection, certain areas warrant an in-depth review and understanding. Third-party risks are a significant concern for organisations that rely on external vendors for data processing, storage, or hosting the AI platform. Understanding data location and movement across borders, as well as collaborating with third-party systems, is crucial for all companies to comply with regulations. Ensuring that these partners uphold stringent data protection standards is essential to minimising exposure. If inadequate due diligence is conducted on a data processor or contractor and a breach occurs which is their fault, and due diligence would have highlighted the fault, the liability would fall at the feet of the data controller. Furthermore, the controller may suffer reputational damage regardless of what due diligence is conducted.

AI systems require tailored incident response strategies to detect, contain, and recover from breaches. Developing comprehensive plans enables teams to react quickly and effectively to mitigate damage, understand the nature of any breach, and ensure compliance with regulatory requirements by notifying the necessary authorities when a breach occurs. Ideally, businesses should run exercises to practice and understand ownership, escalation, damage implications, and accountability. You should repeat this process at least annually and try to review as many scenarios as possible. Companies should be prepared and, when an incident occurs – which may require them to inform the ICO in the UK, or equivalent authorities elsewhere – act within the 72-hour time limit imposed by the GDPR.

Lastly, the environmental impact of data-intensive AI systems deserves greater focus. With growing concerns about sustainability, you can explore energy-efficient training methods and infrastructure powered by renewable resources. Addressing these issues aligns with broader corporate social responsibility goals while fostering a more sustainable future.

In summary, data protection is not just a regulatory obligation but a cornerstone of ethical and practical AI use. By adopting robust security measures, complying with evolving regulations, testing response scenarios, and embracing emerging practices like zero-trust architectures, you can effectively mitigate data breaches. However, be aware that it's challenging, if not impossible, to legislate against all breaches, as this is a rapidly changing area of technology. We have only scratched the surface of data protection here – it's a far-reaching and widely discussed topic.

I highly recommend that you research and seek advice from a professional before embarking on your AI projects. Conducting a Data Protection Impact Assessment (DPIA) and putting in place a Data Protection Officer (DPO), either internally or appointing an external consultant, would be highly advantageous to understand the implications of your data and the projects you plan to undertake.

To help you navigate this complex area, there are specialists in data protection and governance who can assist, offering advice and guidance to ensure you not only meet your regulatory requirements but also understand them thoroughly. It's all very well meeting compliance, but without the understanding, your decision-making process for future AI projects could be brought to a halt before they have begun.

Accountability in autonomous systems

As AI systems become more autonomous and embedded in critical areas of our lives, the question of accountability grows increasingly complex. These technologies are designed to operate with minimal human intervention, which complicates traditional approaches to assigning responsibility when things go wrong. Unlike conventional tools, AI systems can adapt, learn, and make decisions, creating scenarios where it is challenging to pinpoint liability. This issue is particularly pressing as AI applications expand into domains like transportation, healthcare, education, and financial decision-making – where mistakes can have profound consequences. Let's explore a few of these areas and understand the implications and problems that arise, allowing you to consider how accountability needs to be included in your projects.

Autonomous vehicles

The rise of autonomous vehicles has revolutionised transportation, but it has also created significant challenges in determining accountability for accidents. In traditional human-driven cars, liability typically falls on the driver or, in some cases, the vehicle manufacturer if a defect is involved. However, autonomous vehicles, especially self-driving taxis, complicate this framework. Without a driver, liability cannot be attributed to a human operator. This raises critical questions about how accountability is assigned when incidents occur, particularly when these involve loss of life or collisions between autonomous systems.

In the case of self-driving taxis, the absence of a driver entirely removes one of the traditional anchors of liability. If a taxi collides with another vehicle – a pedestrian, or an obstacle – responsibility must shift elsewhere. This raises the question: Should the blame lie with the manufacturer, the software developer, or the organisation operating the fleet? Once the car is deployed, the system's decision-making is typically a product of its machine learning algorithms, which adapt to real-world conditions in ways that its creators may not have explicitly programmed.

In these cases, it becomes increasingly complex to assign liability to software developers, as the AI's behaviours are not solely dictated by initial programming but also by ongoing data inputs and learning processes. This leaves the manufacturer as the most logical entity to bear responsibility. Manufacturers, in turn, must take proactive steps to mitigate risk, such as implementing rigorous testing protocols, establishing robust safety redundancies, and ensuring that their systems comply with both ethical and legal standards.

Another emerging challenge involves accidents where autonomous vehicles collide with one another. In such scenarios, the traditional approach of assigning blame based on human error is inapplicable. If both vehicles are operating under machine-learning algorithms that adapt and evolve independently, pinpointing fault becomes

extraordinarily complex. This issue becomes even more fraught when such collisions result in loss of life.
In these cases, manufacturers may still be held responsible, as they are ultimately accountable for the safe deployment of their vehicles. This accountability includes ensuring that their systems are interoperable with other autonomous systems on the road, minimising risks of miscommunication or conflicting behaviours. Industry-wide standards and shared protocols for autonomous vehicles could play a critical role in reducing such incidents; however, achieving these standards requires extensive collaboration between manufacturers, regulators, and technologists.
In 2018, a self-driving car operated by Uber struck and killed a pedestrian in Arizona. Investigations revealed flaws in both the software and human oversight, highlighting the shared responsibility of developers, operators, and regulators. This case underscored the need for robust testing protocols and clearer accountability frameworks.

Healthcare

The integration of AI into healthcare brings transformative possibilities, but it also introduces significant challenges, particularly in scenarios where errors occur. The traditional accountability frameworks that assign blame to individual healthcare providers are no longer sufficient when AI systems become integral to the decision-making process. This raises a critical question: How do we ensure accountability and trust in a system where human oversight and AI-driven recommendations intersect?

AI's greatest strength, its ability to process vast amounts of data and generate insights, can also be its most significant flaw. Unlike human practitioners, AI systems do not inherently recognise when their data or analysis is insufficient to produce reliable results. They are always designed to provide an answer, even when the underlying information is incomplete, conflicting, or unreliable. This creates a dangerous scenario where the AI's recommendations could be misleading or incorrect, potentially resulting in harm to the patient.

An AI system analysing a set of symptoms might attempt to fit them into a known pattern, generating a diagnosis even if the data lacks clarity or context. This "confidence without certainty" poses a critical risk. A misdiagnosis from AI – presented with unwarranted authority – could lead healthcare professionals to pursue ineffective treatments or overlook critical conditions. The system's inability to flag uncertainty or recognise its own limitations amplifies these risks.

For AI to function safely and effectively in healthcare, it must transition from being seen as an autonomous authority to an intelligent assistant. This involves creating procedural safeguards that ensure AI tools augment human expertise rather than replace it. AI should operate within clearly defined parameters, focusing on well-documented and well-understood medical scenarios

where its decision-making capabilities are reliable and evidence based.
In unknown or ambiguous scenarios, AI systems must be programmed to recognise and highlight their limitations.

- ***Uncertainty flagging*:** AI systems should include mechanisms that flag cases where data is insufficient or patterns do not match known diagnoses. This would alert the healthcare team to investigate further or consult additional resources.
- ***Human-in-the-loop processes*:** Decisions in ambiguous or critical cases should always involve a human practitioner who can assess the AI's recommendations and incorporate their own judgement.
- ***Structured decision pathways*:** AI systems should follow predefined protocols that delineate when to provide recommendations and when to escalate cases for human review.

To establish trust and reliability, clear accountability frameworks are required. These must delineate responsibilities ensuring that errors are addressed systematically and not simply deferred to patients or individual practitioners.
IBM's Watson for Oncology – once hailed as a revolutionary tool for cancer treatment – faced criticism when its recommendations were found to be inconsistent and sometimes unsafe. This raised questions about the

adequacy of testing and the role of human oversight in deploying AI in critical areas.

Professionals in the healthcare sector need to use AI as a supplementary tool rather than a definitive decision-maker. Practitioners must be trained to interpret AI recommendations, understanding their limitations and integrating them into a broader clinical context. Providers have a duty to inform patients about the role of AI in their care, including its associated risks and benefits. Patients should not bear the primary burden of seeking second opinions for every diagnosis; therefore, they must be empowered with knowledge about the role of AI in their care. Transparency about AI's capabilities and limitations can help patients make informed decisions, but this must not shift undue responsibility onto them.

Healthcare organisations deploying autonomous AI systems should establish internal ethical review boards to assess potential risks and implications. These boards can serve as a checkpoint to evaluate whether the deployment of an AI system aligns with organisational values and societal expectations.

The role of stakeholders

Businesses are at the forefront of shaping AI's ethical landscape, wielding the power to influence how AI systems are designed, deployed, and perceived. As organisations increasingly integrate AI into their operations, their actions can either reinforce responsible practices or exacerbate societal challenges. By prioritising transparency and fairness, businesses have a unique opportunity to ensure that AI serves as a force for good. This responsibility extends beyond profit margins; it encompasses the fundamental principles of accountability, and public trust.

One of the most important steps businesses can take to promote ethical AI is building diverse development teams. AI systems are only as unbiased as the data and perspectives that shape them. Teams lacking diversity may unintentionally embed biases into algorithms, perpetuating inequalities. This challenge is already visible in large language models like ChatGPT and Copilot, which have been trained on Western-centric data. As a result, they can interpret the world through a narrow cultural lens, which may potentially misrepresent or overlook values, norms, and practices from other parts of the world. By including individuals from diverse backgrounds, organisations can better anticipate potential areas of weakness and create AI systems that work equitably for everyone. Diversity should extend beyond technical roles; input from ethicists, sociologists, and community representatives can provide valuable perspectives during the development process. This interdisciplinary approach ensures that AI is not just technically sound but also socially responsible.

These guidelines define how AI should be developed and deployed, aligning organisational values with technological innovation. Ethical AI frameworks might include principles such as fairness, transparency, accountability, and privacy. For example, a business could commit to regularly auditing its algorithms for bias, ensuring they produce equitable outcomes across all user groups. Ethical AI frameworks also include implementing XAI solutions. By designing systems that can clearly articulate their decision-making processes, businesses can enhance trust and accountability.

Transparency builds trust, empowering consumers to make informed decisions about engaging with AI-driven services. An e-commerce platform using AI to personalise recommendations should provide clear information about how data is collected and used. Consumers should also be able to opt out or customise their preferences, ensuring they retain control over their interactions with AI.

Beyond individual transparency, businesses can lead broader public education initiatives. Hosting webinars, publishing white papers, or collaborating with educational institutions can demystify AI for the public. Informed consumers are more likely to adopt and advocate for the responsible use of AI.

This proactive approach not only safeguards public trust but also positions businesses as leaders in the evolving AI landscape. When organisations demonstrate a commitment to ethical AI, they set an example for others to follow, ensuring that AI's transformative potential benefits everyone equitably.

The role of governments

Governments have a direct responsibility for how Artificial Intelligence continues to develop and is used, they need to understand how to balance innovation with the protection of public interests. They need to act by setting clear regulatory boundaries and expectations, they have to shape how AI is deployed and ensure it is used responsibly and fairly. Their actions safeguard citizens' rights and establish the foundation for sustainable and inclusive AI development on a global scale.

One of the most critical responsibilities of governments is to enact laws and regulations that address the unique challenges posed by AI. Unlike traditional technologies, AI systems operate with a level of autonomy that complicates accountability and oversight. Legislation needs to establish clear rules for issues like algorithmic transparency, bias mitigation, and liability in cases where AI systems cause harm.

By mandating transparency, governments can make sure that citizens have recourse when they are affected by AI-driven decisions. Liability laws will also need to be updated to account for autonomous systems, defining who is responsible for any incidents, whether it is developers, operators, owners or users. AI systems operate across multiple jurisdictions, making harmonised international regulations essential. Collaborative efforts, such as the European Union's AI Act, represent a necessary step toward creating consistent global standards that protect citizens while fostering innovation.

Explaining AI and building public trust are necessary for ensuring its widespread acceptance and responsible use. Many people remain both wary and confused by AI, associating it with job displacement, surveillance, futuristic or science fiction films. These perceptions shape how AI is received and understood in everyday life. Governments will need to address these concerns through public awareness campaigns that highlight the benefits of AI while addressing potential risks. Still, they will need to do it in an empathetic way to connect with concerned people. Educational initiatives could include workshops, online resources, or media campaigns that explain AI in accessible terms. At the same time, these campaigns should acknowledge and address risks, like bias or privacy concerns, helping to support a more informed and balanced public dialogue.

By engaging everyone in discussions about AI, governments can try and dispel misconceptions and ensure that the technology is implemented in ways that reflect societal values. Public participation in policymaking, like through consultations or forums, further enhances trust and ensures that regulations align with the needs and expectations of the people they serve. When governments enact thoughtful legislation, invest in research, and educate the public, they lay the groundwork for an AI ecosystem that benefits everyone. By striking a balance between innovation and regulation, they can influence AI's transformative potential while protecting citizens' rights and addressing ethical concerns. Governments that take proactive steps to shape AI's development ensure the responsible use of the technology while gain public trust, promote economic growth, and enhance global competitiveness. Too often, though, governments do too little and too late, which in turn leads to public distrust. As individuals, we need to collaborate and ensure that all engagement is inclusive; because only by sharing, talking and listening, can we lead the way toward an equitable AI-driven future.

Researchers and academics

Researchers and academics are at the forefront of shaping the ethical development of Artificial Intelligence. Their work advances technical solutions while exploring the societal impacts of AI. By combining technical expertise with interdisciplinary collaboration, they play a pivotal role in ensuring that AI is developed and deployed in ways that align with societal values and ethical principles.
One of the most significant contributions of researchers is the development of XAI, which aims to make AI systems more transparent and understandable. Researchers are working to overcome the "black box" challenges by designing algorithms that can articulate their decision-making processes in human-readable formats. This level

of transparency will enhance trust but also enables practitioners to verify and challenge AI recommendations when necessary. Prioritising explainability empowers users to make informed decisions and bring about greater accountability within AI systems.

Researchers and academics have recognised the need for interdisciplinary collaboration, bringing together experts from diverse fields such as philosophy, sociology, law, and computer science. This holistic approach means that AI is developed with a deep understanding of its societal implications.

Philosophers can provide ethical frameworks for addressing moral dilemmas in AI decision-making, like how autonomous vehicles should prioritise safety in unavoidable accident scenarios. Sociologists can study the societal impacts of AI – including its potential to exacerbate inequalities or disrupt labour markets. Legal scholars can contribute insights into regulatory frameworks, helping to define liability and accountability for AI systems.

These collaborations enrich the research process, ensuring that AI solutions are both technically sound and socially responsible and ethical. By integrating diverse perspectives, researchers can anticipate unintended consequences and design systems that better align with societal values.

Academic institutions and researchers also play a role in thought leadership, shaping industry standards and influencing policy. Through the publication of ethical guidelines, white papers, and research studies, they provide valuable insights that guide both industry and government in navigating the complexities of AI ethics. Institutions like The Alan Turing Institute and the Partnership on AI have published frameworks that outline best practices for developing and deploying AI responsibly. These guidelines address issues like fairness, transparency, accountability, and inclusivity, offering actionable recommendations for organisations and policymakers.

Contributing to these discussions, researchers help keep ethical considerations central to AI development, rather than an afterthought. Their work inspires public discourse and establishes benchmarks for evaluating the moral implications of AI technologies.

As Artificial Intelligence becomes increasingly integral to society and business, its ethical and regulatory implications demand thoughtful consideration. We've only just begun to explore in this chapter, however, hopefully I have provided you with enough of an understanding of the key challenges – including biases in AI systems, privacy concerns, the need for accountability in autonomous decision-making, and the requirement for robust governance. These issues are not just theoretical; they have profound real-world consequences for individuals, businesses, and society, and you need to consider them when planning any AI project.

Addressing these challenges requires a multi-stakeholder approach. You must adopt transparent practices, embrace diversity in development teams, and implement ethical AI frameworks. Governments have a crucial role in establishing clear regulations that balance innovation with public interest. Researchers and academics contribute by advancing technical solutions – such as XAI – and fostering interdisciplinary dialogue to shape ethical guidelines. Without a proactive approach to these challenges, the trust in and adoption of AI could falter, limiting its transformative potential. At the same time, by embedding ethics into AI strategies and fostering collaboration among stakeholders, you can ensure that AI drives business success while also promoting societal good.

In the next chapter we'll explore the future of AI and its capacity to shape industries and solve global problems. However, the foundation laid in this chapter underscores an important truth: Ethical AI is not an optional consideration; it is the cornerstone of responsible innovation. As a society, we must all leverage AI to create a fairer, more equitable, and forward-thinking future for everyone.

To ensure that your AI initiatives adhere to ethical principles and regulatory requirements, review the 'AI Ethics and Governance Checklist'. Download a copy from www.benjaminrowe.com. This tool provides actionable steps for building transparency, fairness, and accountability into your projects.

Chapter 5: The future of AI

We've covered the past and the present. We're now at a time in history when Artificial Intelligence is no longer confined to speculative possibilities. We are all using it every day, whether we interact with it intentionally or not. It has become a driver of change that continues to evolve and expand its influence across all areas of industry. However, as we look toward the future, the actual realisation of AI will lie in its potential to change our existing processes and redefine them entirely, sparking innovation in ways we never imagined.

Breakthroughs in areas like hyper-automation, quantum computing, robotics, Agentic AI, and sustainability will mark the next wave of AI advancements. They will further embed themselves into complex systems like healthcare, education, and climate change mitigation. The future of AI in our businesses, though, is not just about adopting the latest technology; it's about fostering a mindset of continuous learning, innovation, and adaptability. As AI continues to mature, its impact will not simply be about improving productivity and efficiency, but also about reshaping how we solve global problems.

In this final chapter, I aim to explore the potential of what lies ahead for humans and AI, as well as how businesses will navigate an AI-driven future. We're going to examine some of the emerging trends that will shape tomorrow's workplace, the visionary applications that push the boundaries of possibility, and practical strategies for preparing for these changes. While there are plenty of opportunities, there are also plenty of challenges that require strategic foresight, ethical commitment, and robust collaboration among all of us.

Remember, if you are stepping into the world of AI, don't look around at what everyone else is doing. Focus on yourself and your own business, your own challenges, and lay your own path to lead the next AI revolution.

Buzzwords in AI

Several AI buzzwords are circulating. Some may not be directly relevant to business, but they are more likely to be important in the broader context of AI. Many systems are only accessible through large-scale models. While they can be utilised, it's essential to understand their capabilities and how they can benefit your business, both now and in the future.

Artificial General Intelligence (AGI)

AGI represents the next evolution of AI. Systems capable of replicating human-level intelligence across multiple tasks, not just narrow, specific ones. Unlike current AI, which excels at single applications like language processing or image recognition, AGI would possess the ability to learn, reason, and adapt autonomously, much like humans. This advancement holds enormous potential to revolutionise industries and solve complex problems with creativity and flexibility. However, AGI also raises significant ethical and societal questions, such as how to ensure alignment with human values and maintain control over systems with such immense cognitive capabilities. While still theoretical, AGI remains a key focus for future innovation.

Agentic AI

This refers to AI systems that can take actions independently, pursuing goals or tasks with minimal human input. Unlike traditional tools that wait for instruction, Agentic AI can make decisions, plan steps, and adapt its behaviour based on outcomes. While we're not talking about full autonomy or sentience, the idea of giving AI a degree of agency raises new questions regarding responsibility, alignment, and oversight, especially in complex environments.

Edge AI

Edge AI brings Artificial Intelligence to local devices like IoT systems, smartphones, and sensors, enabling real-time processing without relying on centralised cloud servers. By running AI directly on the "edge" of networks, it significantly reduces latency, improves response times, and lowers energy consumption. Autonomous vehicles use Edge AI for instant decision-making, while smart home devices process commands locally for faster performance. This decentralised approach also enhances privacy by keeping sensitive data on-device rather than transmitting it to the cloud.

Neural interfaces

Neural interfaces, powered by AI, create a direct connection between the human brain and machines, enabling groundbreaking advancements in healthcare and accessibility. These brain-machine interfaces (BMIs) enable users to control devices, prosthetics, or computers solely through their thoughts. For individuals with paralysis or neurological conditions, neural interfaces restore mobility, communication, and independence. In healthcare, they assist in rehabilitation, offering personalised treatments by monitoring brain activity. Beyond medicine, this technology has the potential to enhance human cognition and productivity. While this technology is still in its early stages of development, neural interfaces represent a profound step toward merging human intelligence with AI.

AI and creativity

AI is making waves in many industries – none more so than creativity, as it assists in the generation of art, music, video, and written content. Tools like DALL·E and Midjourney produce high-quality images based on text prompts, inspiring visual artists and designers. In video generation, AI platforms are creating lifelike animations, virtual sets, and realistic simulations, saving time and changing the way filmmakers use creative tools to tell their stories.

While AI excels at generating outputs based on existing data, it lacks the emotional intent and personal storytelling, which are the main hallmarks of human creativity. There is also a risk that over-reliance on AI could dilute originality, leading to output that feels derivative or overly uniform, variations of the same thing, rather than truly unique ideas.
Using AI as a collaborative tool to augment, rather than replace, human ingenuity will become increasingly important. This ensures that creativity does not overshadow artists but empowers them with tools that make imagination more accessible and creation a simpler task. I've used AI to assist in the delivery of this book. Using it to define the foundations and structure, assist in fact-checking, and producing certain content – but the writing, editing, and storytelling are all human-led.

Along with creative potential, there are also significant ethical and legal issues to consider. Many AI models are trained on vast amounts of online content, including copyrighted works from musicians, artists, and writers, often without permission. This has sparked concern across the creative industries, as some feel their intellectual property has been used to build tools that now compete with them. The debate around licensing, compensation, and consent is evolving, and governments and legal bodies are only just beginning to address it. For now, it's a reminder that AI's ability to generate content should be balanced with respect for the people whose original work made that possible.

Hyperautomation

Hyperautomation is the integration of Artificial Intelligence, machine learning, and robotic process automation to streamline complex workflows. Unlike traditional automation – which focuses on specific tasks – hyperautomation enables entire processes to operate seamlessly, delivering efficiency at scale, with potential cost savings. For you, the appeal could lie in its transformative potential; hyperautomation doesn't just replace repetitive manual tasks; it optimises end-to-end operations by connecting disparate systems and enabling smarter, data-driven decisions. For instance, it can automate patient onboarding and diagnostics, allowing medical staff to focus on patient care. Similarly, in a retail environment, an AI-driven inventory management system can predict demand, automate restocking, and reduce waste.

Quantum AI

Quantum AI combines the computational power of quantum computing with the intelligence of AI, investigating solutions to problems that are beyond the reach of classical systems. By applying the principles of quantum mechanics, these systems can process vast amounts of data simultaneously, unlocking breakthroughs in fields like cryptography, drug discovery, and logistics. The potential of Quantum AI is in its ability to solve problems at a scale never even thought possible before. For example, in supply chain management, it could completely change route planning and inventory allocation, significantly improving efficiency. And again, in healthcare, quantum AI accelerates drug discovery by simulating complex molecular interactions, reducing research timelines from years to months. However, as with all new tech, quantum AI is still in its infancy. The hardware remains expensive and difficult to scale, and there's a significant skills gap in this emerging field.

Industries leading the AI revolution

Specific industries are at the forefront of adopting cutting-edge technology, particularly advancements in AI. We've examined industries like healthcare, manufacturing, and finance in detail because they are not just integrating AI into their existing processes but also exploring groundbreaking applications that redefine their capabilities. Their potential to embrace AI and push boundaries serves as a lesson for what's possible, offering a glimpse into the future of how AI will shape businesses and society on a broader scale. To better understand this, let's explore a couple of examples.

Healthcare

AI is reshaping the way we think about healthcare by implementing innovations that go far beyond traditional

applications. One cutting-edge advancement is organ-on-a-chip technology, which replicates human organ functions on microchips. AI analyses these systems to predict how drugs interact with human organs, significantly reducing the need for animal testing and accelerating drug development.
Another promising development is the use of AI-guided surgical robots, which enhance precision during complex procedures. Unlike earlier robotic systems, these AI-driven platforms adapt to real-time changes and so offer customised assistance tailored to each patient's anatomy. To put that in a real-world scenario, AI-integrated imaging during surgery can highlight critical areas of concern, alerting doctors while minimising risks, and improving outcomes. AI-powered digital twins of patients, or virtual models that replicate an individual's physiology, are also emerging as tools for personalised medicine. These twins allow doctors to test treatments in a simulated environment before applying them to patients, ensuring both safety and effectiveness.

Manufacturing

Manufacturing is embracing generative design, where AI creates optimal designs for products based on performance criteria. Engineers input constraints, like weight, material, and cost, and AI generates thousands of designs. These designs can reveal solutions that humans may have overlook or materials that humans haven't considered and to create new ones that don't currently exist. This approach has revolutionised industries from automotive to aerospace, enabling lighter and stronger components.

AI is also driving self-healing manufacturing systems, where smart machines predict maintenance needs and autonomously repair themselves. This innovation minimises downtime and reduces costs. AI-powered 3D printers can detect and correct defects mid-production without human intervention. In advanced factories, cobots (collaborative robots) work seamlessly alongside humans, using AI to learn workflows, adjust movements in real-time, and enhance overall productivity without requiring extensive programming.

Finance

The finance industry is leveraging quantum-inspired AI to tackle optimisation problems like portfolio management and risk assessment. These algorithms emulate quantum computing techniques without requiring quantum hardware – delivering unprecedented speed and efficiency in processing financial scenarios.

AI-powered blockchain analysis tools are a game changer for fraud detection by tracing complex patterns in cryptocurrency transactions, a task too intricate for human auditors. These tools help regulators and financial institutions combat money laundering and fraud in decentralised financial systems.

Education

Education is making good use of AI with emotion-sensing learning platforms, which detect students' engagement levels through facial expressions, tone of voice, and behaviour. These systems adjust lesson delivery in real-time, ensuring content resonates effectively with learners. Another innovation is AI-driven language acquisition tools, like virtual tutors that use conversational AI to provide immersive language learning experiences. These tools imitate real-world interactions, making them particularly effective for non-native speakers.

AI-powered curriculum design platforms are also gaining traction, where systems analyse student performance data to customise lesson plans at the classroom level, enabling teachers to focus on individualised learning paths without additional workloads.

Agriculture

AI-powered soil microbiome analysis is emerging as a game-changer. By analysing the microbial composition of soil, AI systems recommend optimal crop rotations, fertiliser use, and irrigation strategies, significantly enhancing soil health and yield. Also making a big impact are autonomous drones equipped with advanced AI imaging, which can identify crop diseases or pest infestations at an early stage. These drones provide farmers with actionable insights, reducing chemical use and minimising crop losses.

AI for sustainability

Although AI systems have significant transformative potential, they face criticism for their high energy consumption. Training and operating large AI models requires vast computational resources, often relying on extensive data centres. These facilities use enormous amounts of electricity, with a single data centre potentially consuming as much energy as a small city. As adoption of AI increases, so does its carbon footprint, raising concerns about the sustainability of AI itself.

Efforts are underway to address these challenges. Companies are investing in energy-efficient algorithms that reduce computational overhead, enabling AI systems to achieve results with less processing power.

Edge AI which processes data locally on devices rather than relying on data centres, is another solution that lowers latency and energy consumption. Additionally, organisations are moving toward renewable energy-powered data centres to minimise environmental impact, though creating these infrastructures is resource-intensive. For AI to genuinely support sustainability goals, its development must prioritise energy efficiency. Collaboration between technology developers, businesses, and policymakers will be essential to ensure that AI systems not only solve environmental problems but also reduce their own ecological footprint, making the technology sustainable from inception to deployment.

We're now also using complex AI to solve vital problems by creating tools that reduce global carbon emissions by optimising resource use and identifying inefficiencies. There's potential for use in energy management systems – where AI dynamically analyses power grids to balance supply and demand – ensuring renewable energy sources like wind and solar are fully utilised. We are also taking it a step further by incorporating weather forecasting models, enabling power grids to anticipate and adapt to changes in renewable energy generation. By predicting these variables with greater precision, we can ensure that energy grids can store excess energy during periods of high production and redistribute it during lulls, minimising waste and reliance on fossil fuels.

This predictive capability extends to climate modelling, where AI analyses vast datasets to simulate weather patterns and their impact on ecosystems. Scientists are now using these models to forecast extreme weather events, such as hurricanes or heatwaves, which have become more frequent. This information helps governments and organisations prepare mitigation strategies and safeguard vulnerable communities. By combining energy optimisation with advanced climate prediction, AI is providing more information to aid in making the planet a more sustainable place, helping societies transition to cleaner energy systems while adapting to the environmental challenges of the future.

Beyond industrial applications, AI helps organisations track and manage carbon footprints. Platforms powered by AI provide detailed analytics on emissions and offer actionable insights for reducing impact and achieving sustainability targets. As regulations tighten and businesses face increasing pressure to decarbonise, AI-driven solutions are emerging as indispensable tools for meeting environmental commitments while improving operational efficiency.

AI for wildlife conservation

Big changes are also taking place in the field of wildlife conservation. AI is giving us the ability to enable real-time monitoring, data analysis, and protection of endangered species. We are now using AI-powered drones and cameras equipped with computer vision algorithms to scan vast landscapes, detect poaching activity, track animal populations, and monitor habitat changes. These technologies provide conservationists with detailed insights into wildlife behaviour and threats without requiring intrusive methods.

In marine environments, we can analyse acoustic data from underwater microphones to track whale and dolphin populations, identify illegal fishing activities, and monitor ocean health. Meanwhile, on land, systems are using satellite imagery to detect deforestation and illegal land-use changes in biodiversity hotspots – empowering governments and organisations to intervene before irreversible damage occurs.

Another handy application is in predictive conservation, where AI analyses climate, migration patterns, and ecological data to predict species at risk of extinction. This foresight allows conservationists to allocate resources effectively and develop targeted strategies to protect vulnerable populations. AI enhances traditional conservation methods, making the field more efficient and proactive, and offering new hope for preserving biodiversity in the face of environmental change.

Personalised AI assistants

Personalised AI assistants are rapidly evolving – beyond simple task managers – to become sophisticated systems that anticipate and respond to our needs. These assistants leverage advancements in natural language processing, machine learning, and contextual awareness to help us be more productive. For example, when we get in our cars for an upcoming meeting, they predict where we are going and organise the prep. However, as companies increasingly adopt these tools, there is a risk of over-reliance on AI for internal communications, potentially disrupting human connections within organisations.
In their current state, personalised AI assistants are great at managing schedules, automating repetitive tasks, and providing data-driven information to help us improve productivity. A current wave of automation assistants have recently flooded the market which summarise meetings, prioritise emails, predict our replies, or flag urgent issues that require immediate attention. While

these capabilities free up our time to focus on higher-value activities, an overdependence on AI for internal communications can create unintended consequences. When AI takes on the bulk of routine communication, for example, delegating tasks, following up with colleagues, or even drafting responses for us, there's a risk of alienating us from one another. Human interaction is really important for maintaining trust between us and creating an environment for collaboration and cultivating creativity. Removing the human element entirely can lead to miscommunication or reduced team cohesion, and a sense of frustration and even isolation among teams.
To avoid these pitfalls, we must position these assistants as tools to enhance our collaboration, rather than replace it. It should handle repetitive or low-stakes tasks while leaving complex, sensitive, or creative communications to us. You should foster a culture where human interaction is prioritised. Encourage face-to-face meetings, team-building activities, and open communication channels to ensure that AI complements, rather than diminishes, the human element of our lives.

Humans and AI working together

As AI continues to evolve, its greatest strength will lie in complementing our ingenuity and skills, enabling us to achieve results that neither we nor it could accomplish independently. This symbiotic relationship is especially evident in the creative industries, customer experience, and engineering, where AI serves as a tool to amplify our capabilities and help streamline processes.

The future of AI is not about machines taking over; it's about us leveraging AI as a tool for innovation, problem-solving, and progress. And while it brings real value in many industries for the better, there are several areas where I think it's being overused – or applied without sufficient consideration for its impact. In some cases, there's a risk that AI will replace our judgement where it's still needed, or be implemented simply because it can be, rather than because it adds real value. We need to ensure AI works with us, not instead of us, by using it as a collaborative tool that enhances our decision-making rather than replaces it.

Creative industries

AI is becoming a great tool partner for artists, musicians, and marketers, enhancing creative processes while leaving the emotional and conceptual aspects firmly in our hands. Future AI tools will not just generate ideas but offer intelligent feedback, helping creators refine their work. In the visual arts, tomorrow's AI systems may analyse artistic trends to suggest new techniques or colour palettes that align with an artist's unique style. These systems could transform concepts into visual representations, allowing creators to explore ideas more efficiently.

Musicians use advanced AI to compose harmonies, analyse audience preferences, or even adapt live performances based on real-time feedback. Marketers can benefit from AI that predicts consumer responses to campaigns by analysing behavioural trends and demographics. However, AI's role will need to remain supportive, providing insights, prototypes, and tools to enhance creativity, while human ingenuity drives strategy and emotional resonance.

Books that rely on AI-assisted collaboration highlight this balance, as AI can help refine ideas, streamline workflows, and even suggest phrasing. However, the core insights, emotional resonance, and narrative arc come from the creators. For example, I've used AI in this book to organise certain trains of thought, concepts, and expand on specific topics, but the guidance, critical thinking, editing, refining, and ultimately the cohesive voice remain mine. This collaboration (hopefully!) ensures that the final product is not a sterile, machine-generated text, but an engaging, thoughtful resource that delivers a useful guide – one that is both determined by me and interesting to read for you.

As these tools evolve, the future of publishing will see AI assisting authors much more with tasks like research, fact-checking, and even language translation, enabling creators to focus on storytelling and knowledge sharing. Yet, the human touch, creativity, intent, and empathy will always be at the heart of impactful writing, ensuring that content serves a meaningful purpose beyond what machines can replicate.

Customer experience

Future chatbots and virtual assistants will go beyond handling routine queries; they will understand context, detect emotions, and anticipate customer needs with precision. AI systems of the future might integrate facial recognition and sentiment analysis during video calls, offering nuanced support tailored to a customer's emotional state. Imagine an online shopping assistant that can help navigate product options and provide personalised style advice based on preferences gleaned from past interactions.
Despite these advancements, the human element remains essential for building trust between a brand and its customers – enabling an emotional connection. AI can handle routine and transactional tasks, freeing staff to focus on complex issues, empathy-driven interactions, and creative problem-solving. In this future, businesses will need to draw a fine line between achieving efficiency and fostering deeper customer loyalty.

Engineering and R&D

The future of engineering, research, and development is being redefined by AI-assisted tools that empower humans to innovate more quickly and effectively. In product design, AI systems already help engineers create optimal prototypes by analysing performance metrics, materials, and constraints. Looking forward, these tools will become even more predictive by offering dynamic suggestions based on real-time data and environmental conditions.

R&D teams will also benefit from simulations that model complex scenarios, such as the impact of climate on infrastructure or the long-term behaviour of pharmaceuticals. These tools will allow researchers to test multiple hypotheses simultaneously, drastically reducing timelines and costs. However, the final decisions will still rest with human expertise – ensuring that the outcomes align with ethical considerations, business goals, and societal needs.

AI in space exploration

One of the less talked-about areas of Artificial Intelligence integration is revolutionising space exploration, enabling humanity to tackle challenges that were once considered insurmountable. By enhancing autonomy, optimising mission planning, and analysing vast amounts of data, scientists and engineers can explore the cosmos with greater efficiency and insight. These advancements transform our understanding of the universe and also pave the way for unprecedented achievements in space science.

Astro research generates colossal datasets from telescopes, satellites, and space missions, far exceeding the capabilities of traditional analytical methods. AI processes and interprets these data streams, uncovering insights that might otherwise remain hidden. AI-powered systems have significantly advanced exoplanet discovery, analysing light curves from telescopes like NASA's Kepler and TESS to identify planets orbiting distant stars. Machine learning algorithms detect minute dips in starlight, accelerating the identification of potentially habitable planets. AI also processes data from radio telescopes, identifying phenomena like fast radio bursts and gravitational waves, which provide clues about the universe's origins.

By reducing the time required for data processing, AI enables researchers to focus on interpreting findings and advancing scientific knowledge, thereby driving discoveries at an unprecedented pace.

Autonomous missions

AI's ability to operate autonomously has become increasingly valuable in space missions – particularly where human intervention is limited by distance or environmental conditions. Autonomous systems enable rovers, drones, and satellites to navigate rough, complex terrains and adapt to challenges in real-time. NASA's Perseverance Rover uses AI to autonomously navigate the Martian surface, avoiding hazards, selecting paths, and identifying areas of scientific interest. AI-equipped lunar rovers also scout potential sites for colonisation or resource extraction. These systems increase mission efficiency and expand the scope of exploration into previously inaccessible regions.

AI has also played a pivotal role in asteroid sampling missions, such as Japan's Hayabusa2, where autonomous systems collected samples from an asteroid's surface, providing valuable insights into the solar system's formation.

AI is also at the centre of planning and managing complex missions, particularly those involving interstellar travel or multi-phase exploration. It enables efficient use of resources and ensures mission objectives are met under challenging conditions.

AI algorithms are calculating optimal flight paths for spacecraft, reducing fuel consumption and travel time. During these missions, intelligent systems allocate resources like energy and communication bandwidth to maximise efficiency. AI also conducts risk assessments, simulating potential hazards like micrometeoroid impacts or radiation exposure, allowing for proactive countermeasures. AI's contributions to missions like Mars Sample Return, which involves retrieving soil samples from Mars, demonstrate its ability to coordinate multi-phase tasks seamlessly, from collection to transport back to Earth.

SETI: Searching for extraterrestrial intelligence

The Search for Extraterrestrial Intelligence (SETI) has embraced AI to analyse radio signals for signs of life. Human biases and the sheer volume of data limit the effectiveness of traditional signal analysis methods. AI overcomes these challenges by processing data at unprecedented speeds and scales. Machine learning algorithms detect anomalies in radio signals, filtering out noise and identifying patterns that may indicate extraterrestrial communication. These AI systems categorise signals based on characteristics like frequency and intensity, enabling researchers to focus on the most promising leads.

Colonisation of other planets

AI-powered robots can construct habitats on planets like Mars, adapting to local conditions and materials. These systems will also manage life support, optimise resources, and maintain environmental controls, ensuring the safety and sustainability of human settlements.

Space resource extraction

Asteroids and other celestial bodies contain valuable resources, including rare metals and water. AI will identify resource-rich sites, conduct autonomous mining operations, and efficiently transport materials. These efforts could fuel future missions and benefit Earth-based industries.

Deep space exploration

AI systems guide spacecraft through interstellar space, optimising fuel use and adapting to unforeseen obstacles. They also process data from distant stars and planets, helping identify habitable exoplanets and expanding humanity's understanding of the cosmos.

Challenges and ethical considerations

While AI offers immense potential, it also presents challenges in reliability and ethics. Autonomous systems must function flawlessly in extreme environments, where errors could jeopardise missions. As AI gains decision-making power, questions about accountability and ethical considerations in life-critical scenarios become increasingly relevant. Additionally, the high cost of developing and deploying AI technologies in space raises accessibility concerns, with the risk that advancements will be concentrated among a few nations or corporations. Collaborative efforts and guidelines are essential to ensure that the benefits of AI-driven space exploration are shared equitably.

AI is transforming space exploration, enabling humanity to venture further into the cosmos with greater autonomy, efficiency, and insight. From analysing astronomical data to navigating planetary surfaces and planning interstellar missions, AI empowers us to explore the universe in ways previously unimaginable. As technology evolves, AI will play an even more central role in shaping humanity's future in space, unlocking opportunities for colonisation, resource extraction, and profound scientific discovery. By embracing these innovations responsibly, we can expand the frontiers of human knowledge and achievement.

The future of human-AI collaboration

The future of collaboration between humans and AI will be defined by adaptability, innovation, and a shared purpose. AI's strength lies in its ability to process massive datasets while identifying patterns and helping us automate routine tasks. Human strengths, like creativity, empathy, critical thinking, and ethical judgement, are core to these capabilities, ensuring that AI's outputs are meaningful and impactful.

The ultimate goal should be not to replace human effort but to enable it. By recognising the distinct capabilities of both humans and machines, we need to create a culture of collaboration where AI serves us as a partner, and importantly, one that can be trusted. Without this trust in information, the future of AI will struggle to thrive. This balance will not only drive innovation but also ensure that the integration of AI remains aligned with human values and aspirations.

The future is one where we must make AI work hand in hand with us – achieving results that surpass what we could accomplish alone. This collaboration is not just about improving efficiency; it's about finding its potential, and utilising the right tools for creativity, and driving progress across industries and society as a whole.

AI as a tool, not a replacement

At its core, AI should be treated as a tool to amplify human strengths, not a replacement for them. To achieve this balance, we must prioritise transparency and clarity about AI's role, ensuring that *we* retain control over decision-making processes. AI's capabilities are only as good as the data and frameworks provided by us. Businesses and developers must remain vigilant in designing systems that are both ethically sound and aligned with our human values. The focus should be on using AI to remove inefficiencies, expand possibilities, and empower creativity and innovation.

Building a future with AI

The future of Artificial Intelligence in business holds immense promise, presenting opportunities to revolutionise industries, solve global challenges, and unlock growth. From the efficiencies of hyperautomation and the breakthroughs of quantum computing to the sustainability initiatives driven by AI, this technology is reshaping the way we operate and contribute to society. As transformative as AI is, its adoption comes with complexities. Ethical considerations, like mitigating bias and ensuring transparency demand ongoing vigilance. Workforce adaptation is a pressing challenge, as automation shifts job landscapes and necessitates the development of new skills. Navigating a rapidly evolving regulatory environment requires us to remain agile, proactive, and deeply engaged with policymakers. Despite these challenges, the potential of AI to create a better world is undeniable if it's used correctly. Businesses that embrace innovation while committing to responsible AI practices will lead the charge in shaping this future. Collaboration between industries, governments, and academia will be essential to address the ethical, technical, and societal aspects of AI deployment.

The true promise of AI lies in its ability to optimise processes as well as its potential to address our greatest challenges. Whether it's combating climate change, curing diseases, or exploring the cosmos, AI can be a powerful force for good. However, this promise can only be realised through deliberate and thoughtful action.

To prepare for an AI driven future, a more deliberate and structured approach is needed. This means focusing on a few key areas:

- Prioritise diversity and inclusion in AI development to ensure equitable outcomes.
- Invest in infrastructure and upskilling workforces to bridge the gap between current capabilities and future needs.
- Embrace ethical leadership to build trust among stakeholders and foster sustainable growth.
- Collaborate across industries and borders to drive innovation and tackle complex global issues.

The journey ahead isn't easy, but it's full of opportunities. By embracing a vision of responsible innovation, we can leverage AI's potential to advance progress, improve lives, and create a sustainable, inclusive future.

Preparing for an AI driven future:

As AI becomes a cornerstone of our lives, it's clear that its success lies in understanding its potential and taking thoughtful action. I've tried to explore the power of AI, but the real impact depends on how *you* apply these lessons. This book has taken you on a journey through the world of potential of AI, covering its history, strategic planning, ethical implications, and future possibilities. Here's a chapter-by-chapter recap to solidify your understanding and guide your next actionable steps forward:

Chapter 1: The Evolution of AI
We began with the origins of AI, exploring how philosophical questions and early innovations laid the groundwork for modern advancements in the field. Understanding these roots helped us appreciate AI's evolution and the principles that continue to guide its progress.

Chapter 2: AI Today
In this chapter, we looked at real-world applications and the challenges businesses face – ranging from ethical considerations to implementation hurdles – giving you a

clear picture of AI's current capabilities and the importance of using it responsibly.

Chapter 3: Implementing AI in Your Business
We covered the practical steps to integrate AI, focusing on the balance between strategic direction and tactical execution. From defining goals to piloting projects, this chapter highlighted how you can build momentum with AI while mitigating risks.

Chapter 4: Ethics and Challenges
In this chapter, we examined the ethical dilemmas and challenges posed by AI, including data privacy, data protection, algorithmic bias, accountability, and regulatory complexities. We discussed how these issues impact real-world applications and why robust frameworks are essential for ensuring fairness, trust, and responsible AI development.

Chapter 5: The Future of AI
In our final section, we examined visionary applications of AI, from hyperautomation to space exploration, and the collaborations between humans and machines that define the future. These advancements illustrate AI's limitless potential when harnessed responsibly with a brief glimpse of what's to come.

So now you're wondering how you can translate this into real-world actions... here's a quick start guide showing you how to turn what you've learned into practical steps:

- ***Define your strategy***: Start with a clear vision. Align AI initiatives with your organisation's goals and ensure they address meaningful challenges or opportunities. Without a well-defined plan, even the most advanced technology can falter.

- ***Start small and scale***: Use pilot projects to test and refine AI solutions. Focus on areas where AI can deliver immediate value, then expand these initiatives with the lessons learned. Success in AI is iterative, not instant.

- ***Invest in people***: AI thrives when paired with human creativity and expertise. Upskill your workforce, foster collaboration across teams, and create a culture that views AI as a tool for empowerment rather than replacement.

- ***Embrace ethical AI***: Build trust by prioritising transparency, fairness, and accountability in your AI systems. Ethical practices aren't just good for society; they're essential for achieving sustainable success.

- ***Stay adaptive*:** AI evolves rapidly. Commit to continuous learning and innovation, ensure your organisation remains flexible and forward-thinking in the face of change.

By applying these takeaways, you can move from understanding AI's potential to implementing it and hopefully gaining a deeper insight. The future of AI isn't just about technology; it's about leadership, vision, and action. Embrace this journey and help shape a future where AI drives success while upholding human values.

Final Thought

As we stand at the threshold of this new era, the future of AI is a testament to human ingenuity and determination. With the right strategies, and most importantly the right values, the opportunities are limitless and they are within reach. Together, we can shape a world where AI is a force for both business success and societal good, leaving a legacy of innovation and impact for generations to come.

Human ingenuity and AI technology - working together - can bring about a future of endless possibilities.

Continuing your AI journey

Your AI journey doesn't end here. Implementing and leveraging AI effectively is a continuous process of learning, refining, and adapting. To help you take the next steps, I've provided a series of practical guides and worksheets – available for download at www.benjaminrowe.com. They are designed to bridge the gap between theory and practice, enabling you to transform insights into action with confidence.

How to use these tools

Each guide serves a specific purpose in your AI strategy and implementation process. Start by identifying your organisation's most immediate needs. Whether you're assessing your readiness, defining use cases, or building ethical frameworks, these tools provide a structured approach to tackling complex challenges.

The ***Cross-Department Collaboration Playbook*** (p.64) helps you bring teams together, ensuring alignment, clear roles, and shared objectives across your organisation.

The ***AI Roadmap Builder*** (p.66) provides a structured way to translate ideas into a clear, phased plan, aligned to your business goals.

To ensure your initiatives are financially viable, the ***ROI Calculator for AI Projects*** (p.74) allows you to estimate costs, expected benefits, and overall return.

Before committing to delivery, the ***AI Use Case Assessment Template*** (p.80) helps you evaluate and prioritise the most valuable opportunities based on feasibility and impact.

The ***Data Readiness Audit Tool*** (p.82) enables you to assess whether your data is suitable, accessible, and ready to support AI initiatives.

Clear communication is critical throughout the process. The ***AI Stakeholder Communication Guide*** (p.89) helps you align messaging, manage expectations, and engage stakeholders effectively.

As you move into delivery, the ***AI Project Risk Mitigation*** **Plan** (p.91) supports you in identifying, assessing, and managing potential risks.

When selecting tools, platforms, or partners, the ***AI Vendor Evaluation Scorecard*** (p.100) provides a structured approach to making informed decisions.

To build capability across your organisation, the ***AI Literacy Starter Pack*** (p.102) supports training, awareness, and cultural adoption of AI.

Finally, the ***AI Ethics and Governance Checklist*** (p.145) ensure your initiatives are responsible, compliant, and aligned with ethical best practices.

What to do with completed worksheets

Once you've used and completed these guides, they become valuable assets to drive your decision-making and ensure accountability:

- ***Compile results*:** Share completed worksheets with leadership and relevant teams to keep everyone aligned and informed.
- ***Incorporate into strategy*:** Use these insights to refine your strategic and tactical plans. The completed 'Roadmap Builder' can guide timelines, while the 'Risk Mitigation Plan' can shape contingency measures.
- ***Monitor and update*:** AI is a dynamic field. Periodically revisit these tools to assess progress and adjust plans as new opportunities or challenges arise.

By using these tools effectively, your organisation can confidently move from ideas to implementation, ensuring that your AI initiatives deliver measurable results and sustained impact. Remember, these worksheets are not just a one-time resource; they are living documents that will grow with your business and its AI capabilities. They should be revisited regularly – including as part of your monitoring programme – to make sure you hit your defined targets.

Good luck!

And let me know how you get on!

Connect with me on LinkedIn:
https://www.linkedin.com/in/bdrowe/

Via my website: **www.benjaminrowe.com**

Or email me at: **Hello@benjaminrowe.com**

I can't wait to hear all about your AI journey.

Glossary

A

- **AI Governance:** Frameworks and processes established to oversee the ethical, effective, and transparent use of AI systems. This includes defining accountability, managing risks, and aligning AI practices with organisational values.
- **AI Model Drift:** The phenomenon where an AI model's performance degrades over time due to changes in input data patterns, requiring ongoing monitoring and retraining.
- **AI-Powered Neural Interfaces:** Systems that connect human cognition to machines, enabling direct communication with devices or AI through brain signals.
- **Algorithm:** A set of rules or steps designed to solve a problem or perform a task, often implemented in AI systems to process data or make decisions.
- **Algorithmic Transparency:** The practice of making AI algorithms understandable and interpretable to ensure accountability and compliance with ethical and legal standards.
- **Artificial General Intelligence (AGI):** (Also known as General AI.) The simulation of human intelligence in machines designed to think, learn, and solve problems.

- **Automation:** The use of technology to perform tasks with minimal human intervention, driven by AI or robotic systems.
- **Autonomous Systems:** Systems capable of performing tasks without human intervention, leveraging AI to make decisions in real-time based on environmental inputs.

B

- **Bias in AI:** The presence of prejudice in AI algorithms, stemming from incomplete or unrepresentative training data.
- **Bias Mitigation:** Strategies and techniques used to identify, reduce, and prevent biases in AI systems, ensuring fairness and equity in decision-making processes.
- **Big Data:** Vast datasets that require advanced technologies, such as AI, for analysis, storage, and interpretation.
- **Black Box:** A term used to describe an AI or machine learning system whose internal workings are not easily interpretable by humans. While the model's inputs and outputs can be observed, the decision-making process in between is opaque, making it difficult to understand how conclusions are reached.

C

- **Chatbot:** An AI-powered software application that interacts with users via text or voice, often used for customer service and support.

- **Computer Vision:** A field of AI focused on enabling machines to interpret and analyse visual data, like images or videos.
- **Collaborative AI:** Systems designed to work alongside humans, enhancing decision-making and creativity rather than replacing human roles.

D

- **Data Privacy:** Individuals' rights to control how their personal data is collected, used, and shared.
- **Data Protection:** Organisational measures and practices ensuring personal data is securely stored, managed, and protected from misuse or unauthorised access.
- **Deep Learning:** A subset of machine learning that uses neural networks with many layers to analyse data and make predictions.
- **Digital Twin:** A digital representation or simulation of a physical object, process, or system, frequently enhanced by AI for predictive analytics, maintenance, or optimisation.

E

- **Ethical AI:** The practice of designing AI systems that prioritise fairness, accountability, and transparency to avoid harm.
- **Ethical Leadership in AI:** Leadership that ensures AI is developed and deployed with a focus on fairness, accountability, and societal benefit.
- **Explainable AI (XAI):** A subset of AI focused on making machine learning models transparent and

interpretable. XAI provides insights into how decisions are made by AI systems, enhancing trust and accountability.

F

- **Facial Recognition:** A technology that uses computer vision to identify or verify individuals based on facial features.
- **Federated Learning**: A collaborative machine learning approach in which multiple devices or organisations train a shared model without exchanging their local data. Only model updates are shared, preserving privacy and reducing the need to centralise sensitive information.
- **Few-Shot Learning**: A method in which a model learns to recognise new classes or perform new tasks using only a small number of labelled examples. It aims to replicate the human ability to generalise from very limited experience through meta-learning or embedding-based approaches.
- **Fraud Detection:** The use of AI to identify suspicious or unauthorised activities, particularly in financial transactions.

G

- **Generative AI:** AI systems that create new content, such as text, images, or music, based on patterns learned from existing data.

H

- **Human-in-the-loop (HITL):** A model of AI implementation where humans review, validate, or guide AI outputs to ensure accuracy, accountability, and ethical compliance.

- **Hyperautomation:** The integration of AI, machine learning, and robotic process automation (RPA) to automate complex workflows across industries.

I

- **Internet of Things (IoT):** A network of interconnected devices that collect and exchange data, enhanced by AI for intelligent decision-making.

M

- **Machine Learning (ML):** A subset of AI that allows systems to learn from data and improve their performance over time without being explicitly programmed.
- **Natural Language Processing (NLP):** A branch of AI focused on enabling machines to understand, interpret, and respond to human language.

N

- **Neural Networks:** Computational models inspired by the human brain, used in AI systems to process complex data patterns.

P

- **Predictive Analytics:** The use of AI and statistical techniques to analyse historical data and make predictions about future outcomes.

Q

- **Quantum AI:** Applies quantum computing principles to enhance AI performance. The integration of quantum computing and AI to solve complex problems faster than classical computing methods.

- **Quantum Computing:** A revolutionary technology that leverages quantum mechanics to perform complex calculations far beyond the capabilities of traditional computers.

R

- **Regulatory Challenges:** Legal and compliance issues organisations face when implementing AI technologies, including data privacy laws, ethical guidelines, and jurisdictional differences.
- **Reinforcement Learning:** A machine learning approach where an AI agent learns by interacting with its environment and receiving rewards or penalties for its actions.
- **Robotic Process Automation (RPA):** Technology that automates routine business processes by mimicking human interactions with digital systems enhanced by AI.

S

- **Supervised vs. Unsupervised Learning:** Supervised learning involves training an AI model on data that includes known outcomes (labels), Unsupervised learning uses unlabelled data to find patterns or groupings.

- **Sustainability in AI:** Using AI to address environmental challenges, like optimising renewable energy or reducing carbon footprints.

T

- **Turing Test:** A test proposed by Alan Turing to determine whether a machine exhibits intelligence indistinguishable from a human.
- **Transfer Learning:** A machine learning technique that uses knowledge gained from training on one task to improve performance on a different but related task. Instead of starting from scratch, a pre-trained model is fine-tuned with new data, reducing the time and data needed for effective learning.

W

- **Workforce Reskilling:** Training employees to develop new skills required to work effectively alongside AI technologies.

Index

A

B

J

K

L

M

N

P

Q

R

S

T

U

V2_2 – B.L.S.J - 50.2220, -5.3851

9781036962746

BV - #0158 - 030626 - C2 - 197/132/12 - PB - 9781036962746 - Matt Lamination